PARADIGMS
OF
MARRIAGE

PARADIGMS

OF

MARRIAGE

TEN WAYS TO ENSURE AND
RESTORE MARITAL
HAPPINESS: PIT OR
PARADISE

Robert O. A. Samms, Ph.D.

AUTHOR'S NOTE

This issue of Paradigms of Marriage is an updated version of an earlier publication. I trust the readers will enjoy this publication and benefit from its key concepts to guide couples into successful relationships, termed in this book "Paradise."

DEDICATION

This book is dedicated to my wife, Petula (Precious), our four children and their spouses— Richard and Alicia; Tamaylia and Frank; Royland and Shawna-rika; and Sherine and Stephen—who have permitted me to use my private experiences and theirs to ferret out issues that are vital to marital success. I pray for our continued happy relationship as a family as well as for their own success with their families. In this dedication, I am pleased to include my older brother, Keith, who, although never married, discusses the subject with me in as spirited a manner as if he had experienced marriage for a long time; and my sister, Violet, who, after our mother's passing, was mainly responsible for my care during my formative years. My hope is that many individuals and couples will benefit greatly from the strategies and concepts to be found within the pages of this book.

Contents

The Ten Paradigms

Paradigm One: Pit to Paradise
   Happiness denied leads to the pit (pain, problems).
   Happiness delivered leads to paradise (pleasure, peace).

Paradigm Two: Sorting and Satisfying Gender Needs
   Men's needs are very different from the needs of women.
   Denial leads to the pit while delivery leads to paradise.

Paradigm Three: Ten Paths to the Pit
   Criticizing, blaming, punishing, withdrawing, etc., lead to the pit.

Paradigm Four: Ten Paths to Paradise
   Husband or wife dominated relationships lead to the pit.
   Egalitarian relationships (negotiating, respecting, empowering, etc.) lead to
   paradise.

Paradigm Five: Ten Needs of Nature and Nurture
   Some traits are hereditary and others are acquired.
   Identify these traits in yourself and your partner. Prepare to negotiate if
   differences cause conflict.

Paradigm Six: Problem to Solution
   Put into action a three-part solution process.

Paradigm Seven: From Willing to Acting
   Reveal the process of decision-making.

Paradigm Eight: The Debt Trap vs. Financial Freedom
   Debt is the path to the pit; debt free is the path to paradise.

Paradigm Nine: Law of Diminishing Returns
   Know the difference between sex and intimacy.

Paradigm Ten: God's Design
   Men fill the role of leadership, while women provide influence.
   Ignoring the differences leads to the pit, accepting and fostering them lead
   to paradise.

About This Book

In order for the readers of this book to better understand its purpose and organization, let me make a few statements about it. The main purpose of *Paradigms of Marriage* is to promote successful marriages by isolating the key factors which contribute to the success or failure of the marriage experience. I selected ten key factors by ferreting out the main factors which affected my own marriages to Pamela (deceased) and my present wife, Petula for more than forty years and reviewing the findings of some prominent marriage professionals. These ten concepts are not exhaustive but form the basis of many of the issues in most marriages.

A paradigm is an example, a pattern, or a model. The word "paradigms" is used in the title to indicate that I use simple patterns or graphic illustrations to assist the readers to understand more easily the key issues that determine the success or failure of the marital relationship. The paradigms or illustrations are only techniques to simplify the concepts and make them more easily understood and remembered.

Paradigms of Marriage is based on the view that we can isolate the reasons marriages, after an exhilarating beginning, either drift toward pain, pressure, and problems or climb toward enjoyment, pleasure, and happiness. This book focuses on the tension between "Pit" and "Paradise." The ten strategies are presented through repetition of the same diagrammatic pattern. Taken seriously, these ten illustrated strategies should provide significant aid to married couples as well as to single and divorced individuals who hope to be married and develop successful relationships.

Paradigms of Marriage is designed to help couples discover and remain on the path to marital success. The main idea is that most people marry to be happy. When certain negative habits are developed and practiced, they lead the marriage down a negative path to a point I call the "Pit." The married partners experience pain, problems, conflict, and disappointment. They may end up abusing each other, divorcing, or worse. To the contrary, when certain good habits are developed and practiced, the marriage soars toward pleasure, peace, and fulfilled expectations, or "Paradise." In the center is the tipping point, where the marriage is just getting along and may start tipping toward the road leading to the pit or, if the couple discovers strategies to propel the relationship in the direction of marital success, to paradise.

The purpose of this book is to reveal which issues lead marriages to the pit and which ones lead to paradise. Each chapter suggests ways for couples to avoid the pit and achieve paradise.

Paradigms of Marriage is organized in a strictly topical pattern. Each chapter starts with an introductory statement concerning the topic being presented. It progresses with my reflections on our forty two year marriage experience on that issue. Then, I state the problem relating to the topic, following this with the paradigm and its explanation. The final section of each chapter suggests solutions to resolving the issues and fostering marital success.

The basic ideas are drawn from my previously published book *Making Marriage Meaningful* but here a more practical approach is developed. This book, *Paradigms of Marriage*, is the published form of the PowerPoint presentations used in the Marriage Motivational Series. Of course, the chapters flesh out some of the issues contained in the PowerPoint presentations.

See the Website: http://familymarriageconsulting.com/

Introduction

During the past thirty-five years, as I served as administrator, educator (director of education for a private school system), and clergyman, including marriage officer and family counselor, I have encountered many exemplary marriages as well as many troubled marriages. However, during the past few years, I have observed, and statistics have revealed, a significant escalation of marital conflicts and divorce in our society. In Duval County, Florida, where I lived, the divorce rate was about 70 percent. In Quebec, Canada, where I worked for many years, the divorce rate had soared to 79 percent. This means that of every ten marriages, seven or eight would likely end in divorce. The national divorce rate in the United States was above 50 percent. Currently, divorce rates have declined somewhat. Accurate statistics are not kept because of changes in the systems. As my wife, Petula, and I contemplated these grim statistics, we decided to spend the next period of our lives assisting married couples. We felt specially qualified to become marriage motivational speakers since Petula received special training and Pamela and I had experienced forty-plus years of marital challenges successfully, raised four well-adjusted children, and successfully worked together counseling and assisting families. I decided to write a book based on our marriage experiences, including both the positive and negative elements, and to support its themes with carefully researched information from prominent marriage professionals. Subsequently, in August, 2005, the book Making Marriage Meaningful was published by iUniverse as an Editor's Choice title. My idea was to use this book as a guide for our presentations on marriage through the program we developed called Marriage Motivational Series. As I prepared the presentations for the series, I was struck with another idea. Why not find a way to illustrate the key concepts that foster marital success and prevent marital failure in such a manner that the marital strategies hang on these key principles as fruits hang from a tree? The idea occurred to me that since most people marry to achieve and maintain happiness, their satisfaction with marriage is based on whether their expectations are met. Conflicts develop as their expectations are diminished or dashed.

Many couples, including some who go through marital counseling, are not fully prepared for the inevitable clashing and joining of opinions, likes and dislikes, etc., that they must face. Instead of developing strategies to overcome conflicts, they are overcome by these recurring problems. When happiness eludes them, they separate or divorce, usually after much unbearable disappointment and crushing conflict. It is not merely that they don't get along or they discover that they did not love each other. As problems occur, they become increasingly unhappy and conflicts become more frequent and more traumatic.

Rather than experiencing the pleasure of marital happiness, they find themselves enduring its pain. This book reveals the secrets of avoiding marital failure and achieving long- term marital success. I call this relationship experience Paradise.

Chapter One

Love: Pain & Pleasure

Preview

Love is beautiful, appealing, and passionate, but she is also deeply loyal, sincerely unselfish, and enduringly patient. Her gorgeous younger sister, Infatuation, is romantic, exciting, and charming, but she is impatient, focused on short-term pleasure, sex oriented, and selfish. When these two sisters form relationships, Love gives great importance to the quality of someone's character: Infatuation goes for the looks and charm. Because at a distance they appear to be identical twins, they are often confused. In fact, even the experts in such matters have difficulty separating them from one another. *Webster's Illustrated Encyclopedic Dictionary*[1] identifies infatuation correctly as someone inspired "with powerful but foolish and unreasoning passion or attraction." But the dictionary also considers infatuation a synonym of love.

Describing love, Webster's dictionary says it is "an intense affectionate concern for another person," and "an intense sexual desire and overwhelming affection for another person." Isn't that confusing? These descriptions of love sound more like descriptions of infatuation. If experts have difficulty separating these two sisters' identities, how should teenagers and inexperienced young adults know the difference? And many there are who marry Infatuation thinking her to be lasting Love.

Another issue that should concern us is the confusion of love with sex and passion. A young boy who is passionate about a girl he has seen a few times may tell her (if she resists his advances), "I love you. If you love me you will have sex with me." Since she appreciates acceptance and affection, she may be tempted to give in. If she accepts that premise, both of them have been deceived. Hormones, looks, and excitable passions have little to do with true love. Many people, especially men,

---

1 *The Tormont Webster's Illustrated Encyclopedic Dictionary.*

may have passion for women other than the one they marry. Expressing that affection sexually produces problems. Although love involves emotion, it is not based on emotionalism. Love is based on an enduring relationship, not a fleeting passion.

Let me attempt to illustrate the quality of true love as a contrast to the fleeting passion otherwise called infatuation. During the early 1950s two young people met in elementary school. I believe they were in the same class. Though young, they admired each other and later fell in love.

The young girl, named Iris, went off to college in another country for several years. But they kept in touch. While she was away, the young man, who remained in his home district, took a job about seventeen miles away and traveled home once or twice per week. To her disappointment, upon her return Iris discovered that he had let down his guard and had a child with another woman. Rather than abandoning their relationship, they strengthened it by adopting the child and getting married. Iris's father objected to the wedding and did not even attend. He could not understand why she was still attached to her teenage lover, especially since he had not attended college as she did.

But they forged ahead and after establishing their home, they had four more children. With the exception of a brief period when he traveled to England, the young man remained in his job away from home for the duration of his working career. That meant he returned home once or twice per week for a day or two each time. However, he loved his family and cared for them as much as he could. Iris juggled her nursing career with the raising of their five children. Being a devoted Christian woman, she relied heavily on her faith. She certainly needed that source of strength and wisdom since the three boys were influenced negatively by the rapidly changing community and the absence of their father from home so much of the time. Iris was also passionate about serving the ever- increasing needs of those in her district. Fortunately, her two daughters were more cooperative and supportive.

To add to her burdensome challenges, some years later, Iris discovered that her husband had another secret interest that betrayed the sanctity of their relationship. This time, her rival was not only a woman. Instead, he loved alcohol and frequented the tavern and succumbed to unacceptable influences. The discovery of her husband's conduct brought unbelievable shock and trauma to the otherwise peaceful and passionate relationship.

Despite the ensuing emotional turmoil, this committed couple forged ahead together. They found a way to weather the storm. Their close relationship, though bruised and battered, is still surviving, ever since their first encounter as children more than half a century ago. Recently I interviewed this remarkable lady and she shared with me her passion for helping to encourage other married couples who seek her advice. Her husband also has a similar desire to impart the wisdom he has gained from his marital journey.

> Their close relationship, though bruised and battered, is still surviving, ever since their first encounter as children more than half a century ago.

Their experience provides a peek through the prism of lasting love and enduring marriage. This couple's experience also demonstrates that love may begin with the passion of infatuation, but love grows deeper and stronger while fleeting infatuation flounders and fails.

If true love requires time and dedication to develop, is it possible for two people to fall in love at first sight? Some marriage professionals say no. However, I believe it does occur—but it is very rare. Romantic love is based on principles. Hence, it takes some time to gain true understanding of it. Nevertheless, sometimes when two people first meet, they experience a certain flash of attraction between them. While this occurrence may not be love, it may be an indication that real love is possible. When this relationship is explored, it reveals whether there is a basis for love to develop and mature into a solid relationship.

Love may not always begin with that flash of affection. In fact, many times this type of attraction may prove to be infatuation, merely one gland reaching out to another. My belief is that most often love occurs like a sun rising. It is the slow, deliberate development of a sound relationship.

Let me share another story with you. Once a lovely young lady walked down the street. A group of young men standing on the other side of the street admired her as she approached, and one of them was particularly enamored of her. He said, "I bet you I ask her to marry me."

They dared him and proceeded to settle on a bet. As she came closer, he started to cross the street slowly while calling out to her, "Will you marry me?"

The lady stopped, looked him over for a brief moment and replied, "Yes!" They developed a friendship and were married soon afterward. The way I heard it, they lived happily ever after. Should this occurrence assure us that true love really occurs at first sight? Not really! But what it does tell is that love can develop from a first attraction.

> Love may begin with the passion of infatuation but it grows deeper and stronger while fleeting infatuation flounders and fails.

Personal Story

My first contact with Pam was not much different. It was years ago but I remember it as yesterday. I was eighteen years old and had just graduated from secondary school. I had vowed not to get involved with a girlfriend until after col- lege. I had no financial backing for further schooling, but I was determined that nothing would prevent me from going to college and graduating. In those days there were no student loans. I thought a love relationship to be a kind of barrier to achieving my educational goals. I couldn't have been more mistaken.

When I saw Pam for the first time, I was so impressed that I abandoned my plan to postpone romantic friendship. Immediately, I told my friend, Vincent that I must see Pam again. I met Pam while Vincent and I were selling children's bedtime story books, health books, and religious books to raise money for college. I talked to him about her all day. A few days later, I found a way to meet her again. A friendship developed and deepened. The following year, we went off to a boarding college. We took a few classes together and saw each other frequently in the cafeteria and other places on the campus. On February 2, 1964, the week following my graduation, we were married at the Andrews University church in Berrien Springs, Michigan.

Was that love at first sight? I think so. Since our relationship endured, I could say, "Yes!" I was fully convinced at the time that what Pam and I experienced was love, but time has been the test. We had to confirm it through getting to know each other. It was not infatuation because nothing but love can endure the challenge of the test of time. Until her death on February 15, 2012, I loved and admired Pam the way I did in February, 1959.

My marriage to Petula was quite unexpected. We were living in separate countries. Having met her several years before, I was impressed to contact her and ask for a date. She was very apprehensive. Surprisingly, she agreed. However, on that first date, after asking key questions and being assured of the amazing woman she was, I asked her to marry me. She nervously said, "Yes". We began the long road of knowing each other to discover if we made the right decision. We were apprehensive but confident. After being married for seven years, we are still loving each other. However, we had to apply our learned marital strategies. In fact, we read this book together frequently.

Many aspects contributed to our successful marriage relationship. One very significant pillar in the success of our marriage is security. I can't imagine living daily with my wife without being confident in the future of our relationship. I found that even though I may buy "things" for Petula (Precious), there is a void in her that gifts could not fill. Infrequently, she will actually express this in words. She pays far less attention to what I get for her than how I relate to her. In other words, she appreciates the gifts or the carrying out of her requests but her feeling of affection is sometimes restricted until I show a spontaneous flow of affection for her. Sometimes it's just the little things: the tone of my voice, the readiness to perform an act, the giving of a deserved compliment, or even performing an unspoken request.

For as long as I can remember, I have always selected small token gifts for my former wife and our children on weekends and especially when I returned home after being away for a few days. Sometimes, I accompanied the gift with a little note. Yet I must be careful what I write. On one occasion, while Pam was facing a few minor challenges at her school at the beginning of the school year, I wrote her a note just to boost her spirit. It said, "Things only get better from here. I love you still."

Pam asked me to explain "still." I couldn't because I never thought about its impact. Maybe my subconscious was recalling the fifties song:

> "Still, I need your magic touch. Still, I need you oh so much.
> No one can take your place. No one ever will.
> Oh my darling, I love you, love you, still."

All I know is that I meant nothing negative. Unable to explain myself satisfactorily, she eventually took it in good spirits.

Although some experts claim that affection and security are the woman's domain and men respond less to emotional stimuli, I had a different experience. I feel I need Precious' assurances and affection constantly. I feel so much better when I do not have to think about whether or not she loves me. And there have been times during our marriage when I reflected on that deeply. Fortunately, I do not need to think about that frequently.

Problem

The problem for most young people is to understand what love really is and thereby discover with some degree of certainty when they are truly in love. The definition of love is elusive but when love occurs it is accompanied by a ring of certainty that brings with it a clear sense of self-authentication. However, the felt love must be tested by applying reasonable methods. For instance, a married person could conceivably fall in love with a person outside of the marriage. However, he/she would not be free to express that love with this person who is not his/her spouse. Just as we should not steal to satisfy our hunger, or drink contaminated water to quench our thirst, we must place restraints on expressing erotic love. When we fall in love it must be with our heart and our head.

When we fall in love it must be with our heart and our head.

Love needs expression, encouragement, and care to grow. When it is new and tender it must receive nurture and care. It must also be given time to mature. It is possible to love at first sight but that is only the early blush of love.

Even if one falls in love at first sight, time is required to mature it, just as fruit needs time to ripen to be at its best. Love needs to be tested, tried, and proven. If we apply this process to infatuation, we most likely find it will not, cannot, endure.

Even if a relationship begins with true love, it can suffocate and die. The purpose of Paradigms of Marriage is to explore ways couples can avoid the pitfalls of marriage and develop strategies to foster and promote lasting love in their relationships.

The diagram called Paradigm One, is the first of ten which are intended to reveal the main causes why some marriages become destructive and lead to unhappiness and divorce, while other marriages build positive patterns for happy and successful relationships.

Paradigm One:
Pit versus Paradise

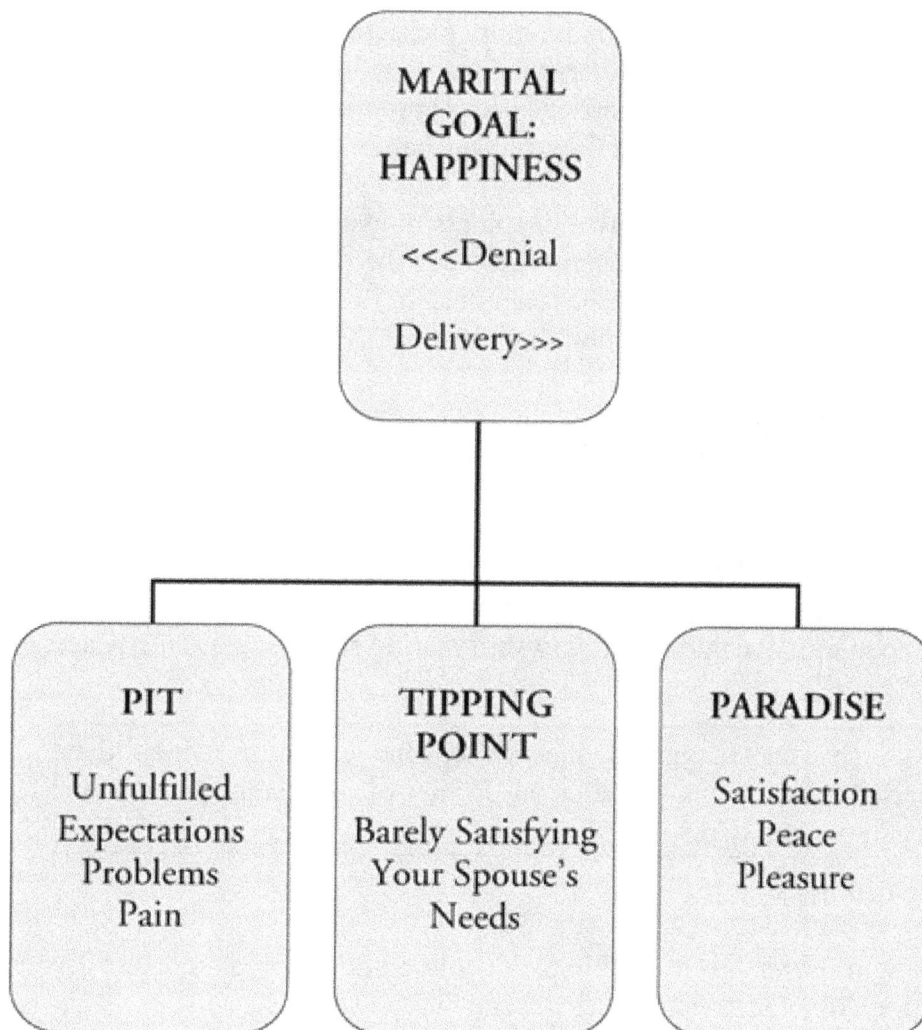

MARITAL
GOAL:
HAPPINESS

<<<Denial

Delivery>>>

PIT

Unfulfilled
Expectations
Problems
Pain

**TIPPING
POINT**

Barely Satisfying
Your Spouse's
Needs

PARADISE

Satisfaction
Peace
Pleasure

Paradigm One Explained

The marital goal of Paradigm One is happiness. Some married people seek to satisfy their spouses' needs, while taking care of their own at the same time. They find a way to meet their spouses' marital expectations. This builds satisfaction and moves couples to the right on the chart, toward pleasure and peace, or paradise. Other people deny their spouses the fulfillment of the expectations they bring to the marriage. Consequently, both partners become unhappy. This leads to painful experiences as they move to the left, toward the pit of despair. Some others find a comfortable middle ground called the tipping point. The marriage is just barely getting along with minimum pain and minimum pleasure.

Married couples seek happiness. If after they marry, they enjoy the experience, their expectations are fulfilled. However, if the marriage proves problematic, they may gradually withdraw, express their frustration by attacking their spouse, betraying their spouse, or taking flight from the marriage.

Instead of concentrating on their own happiness, however, spouses in successful marriages continue what they did best in courtship: They seek the happiness of their partners. They will find that frequently this attention will be reciprocated. Both spouses' happiness depends on the extent to which their marital expectations are satisfied. Denial of those expectations is a deadly marital trap.

Marriages become increasingly problematic as the partners fail to meet each other's expectations, until sooner or later the marriage collapses into pain, problems, and ultimately into the proverbial pit. Some marriages remain in the middle, where expectations are not effectively met or denied. Until those couples can learn to meet the expectations of both spouses the majority of the time, these marriages will lack the luster of their earlier excitement. Other marriages, albeit only a small percentage, foster the achievement of each spouse's expectations. These couples move purposefully toward marital success, pleasure, peace, and paradise.

> Both spouses' happiness depends on the extent to which their marital expectations are satisfied. Denial of those expectations is a deadly marital trap.

Providing Solutions

As the paradigm shows, love can go in the direction of disappointment and divorce or growth and satisfaction. Many married couples depend on hope and good fortune to help them succeed. That's the reason so many marriages end in disappointment.

Marriage requires a lifetime of growth and development. Both partners must make constant conscious effort to achieve success. This chapter merely opens the door to the vast array of issues regarding marital success. Let's look briefly at the importance of security, secrets, and privacy.

Security

In order for love to grow and develop it should be secure. Uncertainty creates lack of trust. Most people who fall in love want the assurance that their partners truly love them and will remain faithful. When security is lacking, doubt develops, and that may lead to unfaithfulness in the relationship. Security is a fundamental need for both men and women. My experience concerning security within our marriage is illustrated in the personal stories above.

However, many prominent writers on marriage relationships relegate the need for emotional security and even financial security to the wife. They consider security a feminine need. Nancy Van Pelt mentions that:

> A woman's need for emotional fulfillment is every bit as pressing as is the male's need for sexual release. It is as unjustifiable for a man to ignore his wife's need for romantic love as it is for her to deny him his sexual urges.[2]

Marriage Counselor David Mace, after pointing out that men seek companionship, a home, and a pleasing wife, says:

> I would venture the statement, however, that the basic drive which impels a woman into marriage is the need for a secure and sustained love relationship.[3]

In my opinion, security is basic for the survival of both wife and husband as well as of the eventual family they may create. Unfortunately, many spouses ignore it to their detriment. You have heard the saying, "My home is my castle." How true! Home should be the place where we find peace, pleasantries, and safety. There *both* partners should feel secure emotionally, financially, and physically.

---

2 Nancy Van Pelt, *To Have and To Hold*, p. 31.
3 David Mace, "The Art of Married Love," in *The Marriage Affairs*, p. 376.

We should not underestimate the differences between men and women with regards to security. They have different needs, and both spouses should try to discover them in order to please each other and enhance intimacies. A wife may seek reassurances from her husband by asking him to do small things she could do for herself. She may expect him to pay certain bills, to purchase the house of her choice, to buy her something she likes, or even to take out the garbage. It's her way of being reassured that he loves and cares for her. His willingness to do these things for her serves to enhance her self-worth, increase her satisfaction with married life, and enable her to be more responsive to him sexually. That's being romantic. When he touches her she feels secure. Nancy Van Pelt declares:

> If a man feels trapped in a bored, tired married life, he might look to
> himself for part of the answer. By consistently and thoughtfully
> expressing romantic love, many men could melt even the most frigid
> wife. 4[4]

On the other hand, a woman should pay attention to her husband's need for security. He just wants to know that she loves him and is completely committed to him. She may give him that assurance in many ways. Being affectionate, responding sexually, and supporting him emotionally will help to fulfill that need.

Emotional Security and Support

All is well when there is peace and security at home. When problems arise the apple cart is overturned and spouses must reach deep within themselves and upward to God for wisdom and support to help them through. During such times of emotional distance, lack of caring, conflicts, stress from children, and financial crises, many families fall apart and separate or divorce.

Emotion cannot be sustained. Nature has provided that it ebbs and flows. We go through cycles of ups and downs. In addition, we change as we grow and are exposed to different experiences and influences within our environment. Yet many spouses do not make the adjustments needed to allow for the changes in their partners. In successful marriages, spouses develop strategies consciously or subconsciously to respond to these changes as they occur. To be successful, we must learn to implement strategies to deal with our family problems and crises.

---

4 Nancy Van Pelt, *To Have and To Hold*, p. 30.

Another Personal Note

It took me many years to figure out that both partners need constant reassurance that their spouse still love him/her. During the first part of my marriage, I did not understand that my wife needed my constant reassurance for her emotional security. Once married, I felt she should know that I love her and that's that. I was wrong. As I discovered late in my previous marriage, Pam needed my expression of love on an ongoing basis. And I needed her assurance that she loved me. Pam was much better at giving me the support I needed.

I learned some lessons quickly but others took years of struggle. We learned to share our life's experiences daily, whether on the phone or in person. And I mean every day. I do not share sensitive information from my work and she does not expect me to do so, but Pam was informed of everything that would help her understand my experience at the time.

Sometimes Pam's experiences at school could be fairly involved. Earlier in our marriage, I would ruin everything by butting in and giving her advice to solve the problem or handle certain delicate matters. I graduated from that a long time ago. Now I listen to how Petula handles the issue or plans to do so and I compliment her if necessary. Occasionally, I do slip up. But I keep it in mind.

In her second day in a new school, a fifth-grade student threatened to slash the tires on Pam's car. She taught emotionally disturbed children in her special education class. This boy rebelled as she was explaining the rules and program for the class for that school term. Pam would have handled the student herself but the class monitor, who was recently assigned to her and was unaware of her ability to handle such discipline, reported the matter to the school counselor, who sent for the student's parents. I was quick to give my opinion of how the boy should be counseled rather than punished to avoid further escalation of the child's reaction. But I caught myself as soon as she mentioned that she was in control of the situation. The next day she reported that the matter was resolved and the boy settled down and did well in her class. What do I know, really? I never taught special education one day in my life. Pam spent half her teaching career in special education and got compliments from all her principals. She did not need any advice from me. She only wanted me to listen. The task of a husband or wife is to listen engagingly and to offer advice only when asked. I count on Precious for her support in whatever I do. She gives excellent support in my ministry. In fact, she serves as the graceful buffer between me and my congregation when misunderstanding arises. She provides the soft side of issues when I try to eradicate programs and plans with other creative ones. Precious helps me soften my radical approach to leadership as I frequently confront issues with a strong leadership style.

I have learned to let Precious know by words and small acts that I cherish her as my wife. We are constantly in touch with each other so that there is no room for doubting our fidelity and conduct.

Secrets

In an effort to be open and supportive, should spouses reveal everything to each other? The obvious answer for most people may be yes. However, consider Andrew Weiner's ideas as he describes them in an article with the title "Shut Up and Save Your Marriage: The Dangerous Myth of Total Communication."[5] He claims no one has actually proved that better communication guarantees better marriages; in fact, he believes that the reverse may be more likely. Open communication may prove to be the quickest possible route to the divorce court. Is that true? Think about it.

I do not believe secrets should be kept from a spouse. However, a spouse may keep personal something that he or she may deem private. A personal matter might be something that, if revealed, would not alter the marriage relationship or create a negative impact. It's merely personal. But keeping secrets from your spouse is the surest way to lose trust should the secret be disclosed unintentionally. Unlike the personal matter, a secret is a fact that might alter the marriage relationship if it were known. If two people are sharing their lives, they should be confident that they will not be surprised when a dark secret about their spouse pops up unexpectedly. When spouses share their secrets, they build trust and security in the relationship. Sharing secrets indicates that the couple has reached a deep level of intimacy in which they feel secure enough to reveal personal and private information to each other.

> Sharing secrets indicates that the couple has reached a deep level of intimacy in which they feel secure enough to reveal personal and private information to each other.

Dr. William Betcher describes the important difference between secrecy and privacy:

> [A secret] is usually provocative, kept a mystery because it might become part of someone else's business. Its content is usually not neutral. Those who share secrets are engaged in a conspiracy of silence, while those who share privacy simply deny intrusion into their closed world. It is possible, however, for something private to be transformed into a secret, and vice versa.[6]

---

5 Andrew *Weiner, Quest Magazine*, Sept., 1978.
6 Dr. William Betcher, *The Seven Basic Quarrels of Marriage*, p. 205.

Although most marriages have both secrets and private matters, successful marriages, according to Dr. Betcher, allow a maximum of privacy and troubled marriages have a predominance of individual secrets.

Privacy is considered "that's my business." It may be withheld from others because if revealed it could prove detrimental to yourself or others. For instance, if the private matter is revealed, someone might be able to use the information against you. Nancy Van Pelt counseled that couples should share anything that would affect the future of their marriage, or, that, if found out, would create trouble in the marriage.[7] Dr. Laura Schlessinger included not sharing secrets with your spouse as one of the ten stupid things couples do to mess up their relationships. Husbands and wives should allow each other the privacy they need, such as a private bank account, private purchases, private space, private correspondence, and private time.

> Husbands and wives should allow each other the privacy they need, such as a private bank account, private purchases, private space, private correspondence, and private time.

---

7 Nancy Van Pelt, *We've Only Just Begun*, p. 187.

Chapter Two

Commitment

Preview

Why do people marry? Why do you or I consider marriage as important in our lives? Why do we want our children to marry? Ever give it a thought? No doubt there are many answers. Likely most of those answers are derived from one main purpose.

Marriage brings us happiness. We want happiness for ourselves and our children. That's the reason religious people desire heaven rather than hell. People are more likely motivated by the offer of pleasure and the avoidance of pain. Even when we choose a painful path, if the end has a purpose that brings satisfaction or pleasure, we embrace it. A mother's painful delivery of her baby and a soldier's willingness to go boldly into battle illustrate that point.

Aristotle, the Greek philosopher, is credited with saying, "Happiness is the meaning and the purpose of life, the whole aim and end of human existence."

In his article on the subject, Richard Harlicks credits Aristotle with the claim that happiness is the only thing that humans pursue for its own sake; everything else we do is aimed at achieving happiness.[8] You may choose to debate whether the pursuit of happiness is the chief motivation for getting married. But I trust you will agree that happiness plays a prominent role. In my thirty-plus years of marrying couples, I can't recall an unhappy couple at the altar. Most people regard the wedding day as the most exhilarating one of their lives or at least one of the most enjoyable. See how you feel about this statement by Dr. John Jacobs.

> We live in a society that promotes so many powerful lies about
> marriage, so many misunderstandings, myths and fairy tales that
> they have

---

8 Richard Harlicks, *Atlanta Journal-Constitution*, March 27, 2005.

become so deeply entrenched in our minds that we are
rarely able to approach marriage with reasonable expectations.[9]

Dr. Jacobs points out that forty years ago, forces in society such as "longer life spans, increased standards of living, women's increased economic independence, belief in the right to personal freedom and happiness, and social acceptability of divorce" did not change "the very meaning of marriage and the stability of marital relationships."[10] Today, they do. He concludes that the only cohesive force holding marriages together today is the quality of the relationship between the spouses.

The point is: The more we rely on marriage to fulfill our desire for happiness, the greater the disappointment if it fails to deliver. Where else would we look for the cause of the significant increase in the divorce rate?

DIVORCE RATE: UNITED STATES
Rate per 1,000 Population[11]

	Marriages		Divorces	
1950	11.1		2.6	23%
1960	8.5		2.2	
1970	10.6		3.5	
1980	10.6		5.2	
1990	9.8		4.7	
2000	8.2		4.1	
2002	7.8		4.0	51%

United States national divorce rate has jumped from 23 percent in 1950 to 51 percent in 2002.
Currently, in Canada, about 4 out of every 10 marriages end in divorce.
Quebec has the highest divorce rate in Canada among the provinces. The chart below shows a comparison of divorce rate in Canada with the United States during a similar period.

---

9 John W. Jacobs, "7 Myths That Can Kill your Marriage," *Psychology Today*, March/April, 2004.

10   John W. Jacobs, Ibid., *Psychology Today*, March/April, 2004.

11 U.S. Census Bureau, *Statistical Abstract of the United States*, 2004–2005.

DIVORCE RATE: CANADA
Rate per 1,000 Population[12]

	Marriages	Divorces
Canada 49%	145,048	70,828
Alberta 45%	17,699	7, 960
Ontario 44%	63,187	27,513
Quebec 79%	21,157	16,738

Divorce rates in Canada are close to those of the United States but notice the exceptionally high rate of divorce in Quebec. I lived and worked in Quebec for about fifteen years. I found that in most of North America, the clergy marriage officers assist the government with the legal requirements of marriage. During my years in Quebec, the clergymen were marriage officers and were fully responsible for the registration of marriages. They issued legal certificates of marriages, births, and deaths. In spite of the influence of the clergy, the divorce rate in Quebec is still the highest in Canada.

Romantic vs. Traditional Marriages

We have reason to believe that the modern American view of marriage has changed. This may have opened the door for the damaging influence of other forces in the society. In a review of the evolution of marriage, John Townsend points out one factor that should cause us to stop and think. He claims that "in all societies through history the fundamental basis of marriage has been a contract between two family lines that have assigned rights and duties concerning property and children."[13]

Dr. John Townsend claims that with the exception of a few earlier cultures, American society is alone in using romantic love as a sole basis of marriage. Until the eighteenth century, romantic love played a minor role in European marriages.

> The primary purpose of the traditional marriage was to produce the
> next generation and transmit to it property, position, and knowledge. [14]

---

12 Source: *Statistics Canada*: 2004.

13 John Townsend, *What Women want, What Men Want*, p. 165.

14   John Townsend, Ibid., p. 165.

Individual feelings were not the most important. Roles of men and women were clearly defined. Husband and wife were largely dependent on each other for operating a successful home. This is closer to the biblical view of marriage where families participate in the selection of the spouse and the marriage process. Today in America, parents are fortunate if their son or daughter asks their opinion before they get engaged. We may credit the sexual revolution for this radical change.

So, we have now transitioned into the age of romantic marriages. No longer do husbands and wives have prescribed roles or functions in a marriage. The line of a popular song incorrectly portrays marriage in the words, "All you need is love." It used to be said that in traditional marriages people marry and fall in love. Today, people fall in love and marry.

In so doing people marry to fulfill each other's needs whatever those needs are perceived to be. Happiness depends on a spouse that fulfills our p erceived n eeds. Often that subjects the marriage to constant review in the mind of the spouse. Is he/she fulfilling my n eeds? D id I m arry t he r ight p erson? S hould I e nd t his a nd t ry a gain t o find my soul mate? Hollywood saturates us daily with its glamorized view of sex and marriage. Combine that with the permissive influences in our society which had their roots in the 1960s, and we have to wonder how well-intentioned couples manage to survive.

> The desire to maintain the sky-high expectation that marriage will fulfill our emotional needs on an ongoing basis is bound to clash with a harsh reality sooner rather than later.

The desire to maintain the sky-high expectation that marriage will fulfill our emotional needs on an ongoing basis is bound to clash with a harsh reality sooner rather than later. Sociology professor Paul Amato makes the point that the practical benefits of marriage used to be foremost in the minds of couples. He writes, "The idea of marriage as a vehicle for self-fulfillment and happiness is relatively new."[15]
He says that surveys of high school and college students fifty to sixty years ago found that most wanted to be married in order to have children and own a home. Youth today want to get married for love. Dr. Amato states, "This increased emphasis on emotional fulfillment within marriage leaves couples ill prepared for the realities they will probably face."[16]

---

15 Paul Amato, *Psychology Today*, March/April, p. 38.
16 Paul Amato. Ibid., p. 38.

Personal Story

When young couples place commitment at the foundation of a lasting relationship, they recognize the need to prepare for marriage seriously. Of course, we should acknowledge the importance of indispensable divine intervention as supreme.

Pam and I expected challenges. Being completely committed to each other provided the firm foundation we needed to deal with the unexpected. Pam and I were Christian youth when we met. She grew up in a Christian home with strict parental supervision. I had exposure to Christian upbringing but had attended a highly secular boys secondary boarding school which fostered a pleasure oriented lifestyle. The summer following my graduation, a schoolmate and I decided to become Christians. This was about a year and a half before I met Pam. When Pam and I began our five-year friendship, we were already committed to the strong religious principles of the church, and we never capitulated to secular desires nor abandoned our religious principles. Our beliefs influenced our relationship. Because of those firm beliefs, we entered into an unspoken commitment as soon as we felt we were serious about each other.

It was that commitment that provided the foundation for our marriage during the dark and difficult days. We burnt our bridges behind us and provided no easy escape route. Before we got married on February 2, 1964, we did not seriously discuss where we would live, the number of children we wanted, the amount of money we needed, or what we owned. We saw marriage as a permanent lifetime commitment, a lifetime bond, and we were embarking on that journey together.

We had no idea of the dramatic changes and incredible experiences that would break upon us during the next forty and more years. The challenges were many and varied. Because of my adventurous spirit and Pam's willingness to share the adventures (most of the time), our marriage was truly a roller coaster ride. The two years preceding our wedding we were both students in college away from home. After marriage we had to pass through the stages of growth into maturity. We had no parental assistance and no relatives or close friends to offer guidance or give suggestions. This means that many changes occurred and we had to cope with them together. After marriage, we moved to Edmonton, Alberta.

Problem

Should marriage be compared to a completed house ready to be occupied or to the design of a house ready to be built? I choose the latter. I believe that the house you will occupy in later years is to a great extent the one you build together. The success or failure of a marriage is seriously affected by the input both partners will make.

If poor quality materials are used or the house is built upon a poor foundation, major problems lie ahead. However, if couples take care during the early phases of the relationship to create a solid base, they will enjoy the positive results that will accrue. My experience has taught me that valuable lesson.

Problems may be inevitable, but fortunately, solutions can be found for many troubled marriages. We must do the hard work of analyzing the causes of problems before we can apply a viable solution. It took me many years and many painful experiences to discover what I should chave known from the beginning of our marriage: It's more difficult to change hardened habits later. However, applying the appropriate techniques, a successful relationship can be deve-loped and problems can be overcome.

> We must do the hard work of analyzing the causes of problems before we can apply a viable solution. It took me many years and many painful experiences to discover what I should have known from the beginning of our marriage: It's more difficult to change hardened habits later.

The marriage process passes through three main stages. Before we view these stages briefly, consider the potential obstacles couples face when they get married. You may wish to add to the list below from your own experience. The following quotation is from my previous book, *Making Marriage Meaningful.*

The fact that both bride and groom were born and bred in completely different circumstances and environments is rarely taken seriously or even considered. Their parents likely shared different values and subjected them to different training and discipline. During their years of schooling, they likely had different friends, thereby being exposed to different influences. In some cases, they were affiliated with different religions and accepted or rejected different doctrines. The profound impact of culture, race, politics, and language on individuals should be taken into account. These factors, along with moral training or lack thereof, could lead to different dormant, deep-seated personality traits. We could even add the potentially devastating effects of heredity or predisposed illnesses psychological, physical, or emotional to which many people are subjected. Then there are the suppressed childhood traumas and various phobias. What of strong likes, dislikes, desires, prejudices, and ambition or lack of ambition! What if any of these influences, or a combination of any number of them, surfaces early or late in the marriage, especially at an unwelcome, critical, or embarrassing moment?[17]

The problem is obvious. Even though the effects of these and/or other influences on a marriage may be clearly evident,

> "we usually ignore them and proceed with our relationships somewhat oblivious to their incalculable impact. The result is frequently a futile fight for marital survival."[18]

The Three Stages of Marriage

Marriage passes through three main phases.

1.Mutual Enjoyment

This honeymoon phase is the period of blind love. The partners see each other as beautiful and charming and the world around is bright and beautiful. They deny reality, and overlook or minimize each other's faults. This period usually lasts only a few months.

2.Mutual Adjustment

As soon as reality begins to phase in, the honeymoon begins to phase out. Each partner's personality traits start to emerge. As they discover their different likes and dislikes or failures and faults, partners may become disillusioned. Wives may feel their husbands take them for granted. Husbands may react to the loss of freedom, new household obligations, and the burden of financial worries. During this phase many breakups occur. Those who endure may enter the third phase or linger in this phase in conflict and disagreement.

3.Mutual Fulfillment

The marriage is now entering the grown-up phase. The partners learn to accept each other, communicate, and develop strategies to resolve disagreements. They develop a bond and trust in each other.

Why do so many marriages fail? Many factors contribute. Nancy Van Pelt attributes failure to lack of preparation. People tend to ignore the complexity of

---

17 Robert Samms, *Making Marriage Meaningful*, p. 14.
18 Robert Samms, Ibid., p. 14.

marriage. Many people believe marriage is a lifelong quest for happiness and bliss. Soon their hopes are dashed. Marriage is demanding. It calls for knowledge, combined with effort, maturity, and patience in order to achieve the reward it offers. It also requires guidance and support.[19]

Eric Cohen and Gregory Sterling support the view that preparation is the key to marital success.[20] They compare emotional debt to financial debt. Both must be contemplated before they are incurred. Most married couples do not clarify their expectations before the wedding. Eric Cohen and Gregory Sterling mention that when married partners fail to meet each other's perceived expectations, conflict begins. This leads to broken hearts and shattered relationships.

> Most married couples do not clarify their expectations before the wedding. This leads to broken hearts and shattered relationships.

Jim Conway places time at the head of the list for marriage renewal.[21] Lack of time is the excuse for lack of effort in working on challenging issues. Whether early or late in the marriage, partners must commit time to listen to each other and learn more about the spouse's needs and desires. Dr. Fred Lowery adds this:

> I want to be gut-level honest with you: Maintaining a loving, intimate
> relationship between two selfish and imperfect human beings is the
> most difficult, most complex, and most time-consuming challenge any
> of us will face in this lifetime.[22]

Marriages fail because every couple faces different sets of challenges and has a different type of preparation. Creativity and hard work are required to build a successful relationship and fewer than 50 percent of us are willing to tackle this difficult task in order to achieve success. Success is possible. My presentations are aimed at providing pointers to the path of marital success.

So far, we have talked about the nature of the problems. Let's consider some preventive or remedial approaches.

---

19 Nancy Van Pelt, *We've Only Just Begun*, p. 21.
20 Eric Cohen and Gregory Sterling, *You Owe Me*, pp. 7, 18, 19.
21 Jim Conway, *Men in Midlife Crisis*, pp. 209, 210.
22 Fred Lowery, Covenant Marriage, p. 109.

Marriages fail because every couple faces different sets of challenges and has a different type of preparation. Creativity and hard work are required to build a successful relationship and fewer than 50 percent of us are willing to tackle this difficult task in order to achieve success.

Paradigm Two:
Sorting and Satisfying Gender Needs

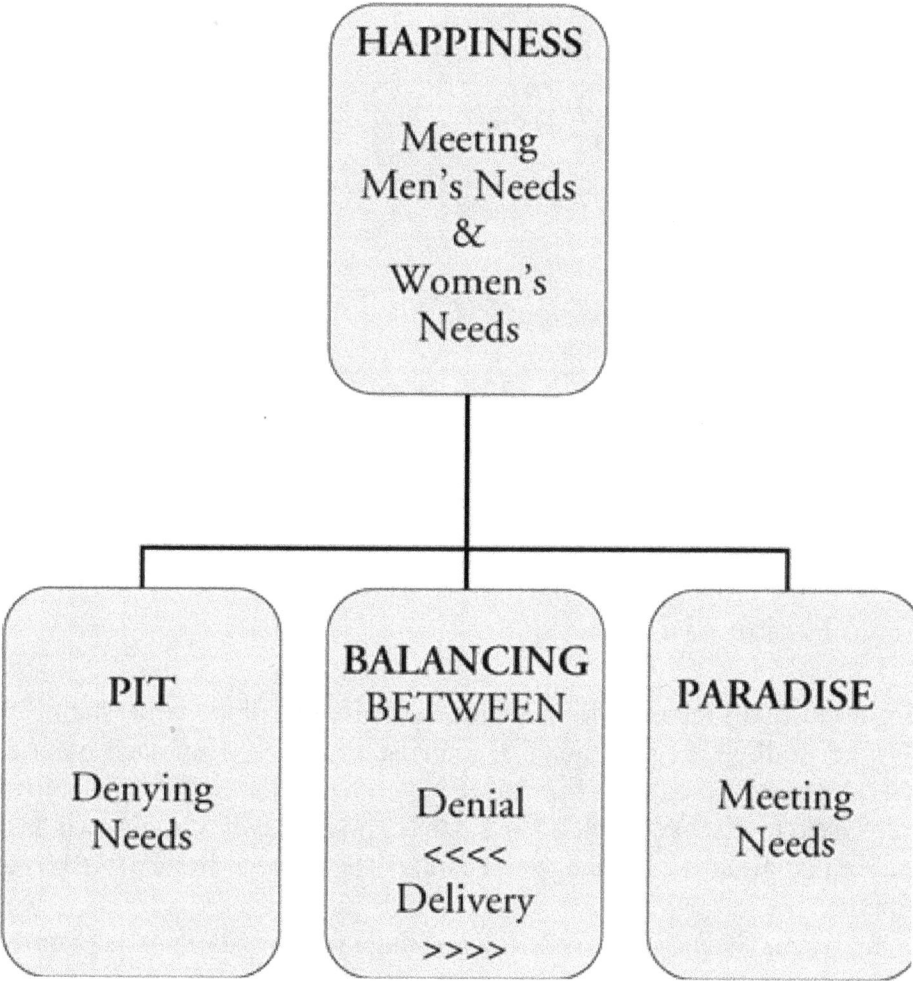

HAPPINESS

Meeting
Men's Needs
&
Women's
Needs

PIT

Denying
Needs

**BALANCING
BETWEEN**

Denial
<<<<
Delivery
>>>>

PARADISE

Meeting
Needs

Gender Needs

Men's Need	Women's Needs
Authority	Love, adoration
Sexual fulfillment	Influence
Attention	Intimacy
Love	Security
To solve problems	To love someone
Confidence	Conversation
Peace	Self-esteem

Paradigm Two Explained

This paradigm illustrates the need for husband and wife to acknowledge their differences and support each other in their areas of need. If marriage partners deny each other's needs, they face disappointment and difficulty. If they meet each other's needs, they can enjoy marital happiness. Couples need to discover each other's needs and the level of their own desire to satisfy them. Remember that these needs change constantly. The diligent spouse will pay attention and make adjustments.

As spouses neglect or deny the needs of the marriage partner, the marriage moves to the left on the diagram, i.e., toward the pit. As they discover and satisfy the needs of each spouse, the marriage moves to the right on the diagram, i.e., toward satisfaction or paradise.

Any casual observer will notice that there are differences between the sexes. However, it takes the keen observer to ascertain how these differences affect marriages and the strategies needed to allow these differences to complement rather than conflict with each other in the marital relationship. Above is a list of the seven leading factors that affect men and women in marriage. Notice that, unlike the list for nature and nurture, they are different for men and women.

Some of the issues listed for men and women have the same title. However, the same perceived needs have different responses in men or women. For instance, both men and women need security. But the security men desire is far different from that of women. Both sexes need love. Nevertheless, they express love in vastly different ways. The key to this paradigm is for husbands and wives to explore the needs of their marriage partners. Once they understand what those needs are, they can begin to discover how they can best satisfy them.

I have attempted to list these needs for both men and women in a hierarchical pattern, that is, listing them from top down in order of their importance to each of the two genders. It is very important to observe that your husband or wife may require a different order for his/her needs. In other words, although most women will choose the need to be loved and adored as most important, your wife may require security most. Furthermore, over time these needs may move up or down the list for individuals as circumstance and maturity create the need for changes. Spouses must, therefore, remain fully alert to the ever-changing needs of their partners.

As you give support to the needs of your spouse, your marriage becomes increasingly satisfying and moves toward paradise. The contrary is true. As these needs are denied or ignored, the marriage experience becomes less satisfying. Irritating issues develop and quarrels occur with increasing intensity. This path leads inexorably toward the pit. Always bear in mind that it is futile to try to get your spouse to think and act as you do. You are by nature and nurture much different from each other. This will remain true despite your effort to achieve compatibility or your feeling that you are compatible.

> Always bear in mind that it is futile to try to get your spouse to think and act as you do.

Providing Solutions

Commitment to the marriage is the first major step, regardless of the trials and heartaches you have experienced in the past or the hopelessness you may have felt. Ask yourself: Is there any life left in my marriage any life at all?

If the answer is yes, let's begin. If it is no, you may still try to learn where your marriage failed so you can look to the future with hope. You may even help your child or someone else avoid serious pitfalls in their marriage.

> Having committed to make the marriage succeed, you need to recognize that there are fundamental differences between the sexes that we must recognize and seek accommodation.

Having committed to make the marriage succeed, you need to recognize that there are fundamental differences between the sexes that we must recognize and seek accommodation. Trying to make your husband/wife act or think in the pattern of your gender is a futile fancy and will lead to frustration and conflict.

Commitment Phobia

For several reasons, some men and some women cannot commit. Certain psychological barriers prevent them from making a long-term commitment to a relationship. Many people are tricked into feeling they can change the commitment-phobic partner once they get married. Be wary!

Commitment means "the state of being bound emotionally and intellectually to a way of thinking or course of action."[23] In the case of marriage, a long-term pleasant experience requires flexibility, adaptation, forgiveness, growth, and a willingness to endure various vicissitudes. With the exception of violence, adultery, or abandonment, the marriage commitment should be for keeps. That's the reason people start with a vow and a legal marriage contract. Human beings are at times vacillating and fickle.

> In the case of marriage, a long-term pleasant experience requires flexibility, adaptation, forgiveness, growth, and a willingness to endure various vicissitudes.

Alistair Begg states:

The vows become very important. They provide walls of protection when emotional winds and waves begin to beat upon the relationship. The traditional vows have stood the test of time because they aptly summarize the commitment that is involved.[24]

Commitment may be considered in four ways: Dedication, constraint, covenant, and contract.

---

23 *Webster's Illustrated Dictionary*
24 Alistair Begg, *Lasting Marriage*, p. 73.

Dedication and Constraint

Dedication is the basis for a successful marriage relationship.

The partners are imbued with an intrinsic desire not only to continue the relationship but to improve it, to sacrifice for it, to invest in it, to link personal goals to it, and to seek the partner's welfare, not simply one's own. [25]

Commitment by constraint refers to forces that obligate the partners to remain in the relationship whether or not they are dedicated. Constraint fosters negative forces which in turn lead to unhappiness, dissatisfaction, and lack of freedom. Many marriages start out as dedication but when reality brings pressure on the relationship, one or both partners switch to constraint. They are disenchanted with the marriage but certain considerations restrain them from abandoning ship. So, they find a new way to cope. They end up in a survival mode. They avoid the pit of despair but fail to advance to the pleasure of intimacy.

Covenant and Contract

A covenant is different from a contract. Both are used in a wedding. However, in a Christian wedding the covenant and contract are separated by the law of the state. The state requires a contract. The church, which performs the wedding, requires a covenant a vow made before God, by both parties. According to Dr. Fred Lowery, a contract is an agreement based on lack of trust. The parties set limits on their responsibilities, their rights, benefits, duration, liability, and they even set an escape clause. A covenant is based on trust, love, and loyalty and sets no limit to the partners' own responsibility.
A covenant marriage is unconditional, unlimited, and unending.
A covenant marriage is more about trust than terms, more about character than convenience, more about giving than receiving.[26]

To be successful, a marriage may begin with a contract or a covenant, but it must be sustained by a covenant.

---

25 Stanley Scott, et al., *A Lasting Promise; The Heart of Commitment*, p. 164.
26 Lowery, *Covenant Marriage*, p. 12.

Since the North American marriage procedures are rooted in biblical concepts, we may look to the Bible for further clues to the true meaning of covenant. The Bible relied heavily on the term and the concept of covenant, mentioning the term over three hundred times in the Old Testament. Genesis 2:24 states, "Therefore a man leaves his father and his mother and cleaves to his wife, and they become one flesh." This divine declaration provided the pattern for subsequent marriages.

In the prologue to their book, Good Marriages Don't Just Happen, authors Catherine and Joseph Garcia-Pratts tell their story. Pointing out that currently people approach marriage as a business venture, they proceed to show how their experience was different. The popular approach in our society is to have a contract duly signed before witnesses with stipulations made and expectations defined, i.e., a marriage contract, in case one party fails to live up to his/her part of the agreement. Rather than a contract, they claim, the Garcia-Pratts approach marriage as a covenant made with each other as a permanent unconditional commitment. They write:

> We chose to be with each other in a never-ending relationship. We chose to love the other in a relationship that would strive to make each of us better individuals. We also chose to integrate God into all aspects of our lives, not understanding at the time of our wedding how integral God's love and spirit would be in the growth of our relationship. We've experienced the richer and the poorer, the good times and the bad, health and illness, sadness and joy, fulfillment and disappointments. The commitment we both made to our relationship enabled us to weather the hard times and grow stronger in our love. Building a loving, lasting, joy-filled relationship entails effort and a constant commitment by both spouses. Good marriages don't just happen.[27]

Iris Krasnow also developed some sound advice for us after difficult experiences, hard work, and tears.

> Yet, my fantasy of marriage as a wellspring of contentment has completely disappeared, and so should yours. Thinking you get happiness ever after is a ticket to divorce.

---

27 Catherine and Joseph Garcia-Pratts, M.D., *Good Marriages Just Don't Just Happen*, pp. 10, 11.

She learned four things:
   1. Marriage can be hell;
   2. The grass is not greener on the other side;
   3. Savor the highs, because you can count on one thing the dips
      are just around the corner;
   4. Nobody is perfect, so you may as well love the one you're with.

She confesses:
   I surrender to this imperfect marriage, because I love it more
   than I hate it and I am committed to this man with a promise
   that I need to, we all need to, do our best to fulfill.[28]

---

28 Iris Krasnow, Surrendering to Marriage, p. 3.

Chapter Three

Conflict

Preview

 Bill Knott, in an editorial for the journal Advent Review, relates a touching experience he had upon visiting an old graveyard near the Vermont/Massachusetts border. He observed graves with obelisks of white marble from the 1830s and slate and granite stones from the Revolutionary War as well as more recent memorials from the Vietnam War. On one gravestone he read the shocking words, "Captain John Parker, 43, July 25, 1786. Accidentally shot by one of his own men."[29]
 When we are with family, we should feel safe. How tragic then that frequently spouses give way to anger or, because of error due to ignorance, they injure the person they claim to love dearly. We should take care to protect the one we love in order that no harm may befall him/her.

The opening statement in the book, The Seven Basic Quarrels of Marriage, says:

Falling in love makes a man and a woman discover how much they have in common. Living together makes lovers realize how many things there are to divide them.[30]

Dr. John Gottman says of conflicts that occur in marriage:

It is as though some powerful, subterranean current takes hold of you both and leads you down a path of negative thinking, destructive feelings, painful action and reaction, drifting toward isolation and loneliness.[31]

---

29 Robert Samms, *Making Marriage Meaningful*, p. 35.
30 William Betcher and Robie Macauley, *The Seven Basic Quarrels of Marriage*, p. 1.
31 John Gottman, *Why Marriages Succeed or Fail*, p. 14.

After the wedding and honeymoon, couples must settle down to a normal day to day life. That's when the proverbial rubber meets the road. The early excitement of love soon dissipates for many couples and is replaced by anger, resentment, and conflict. This is not because they suddenly stop loving each other; rather their love must face the reality of life's challenges. They embark on the never-ending path of adjusting to each other.

Are there ways of determining which couple will succeed or fail? Dr. John Gottman says yes! After decades of scientific research on what makes marriages last, he claimed that he could predict marriage outcomes to 94 percent accuracy. We do not have to be psychotherapists to benefit greatly from the expertise of professionals who spend time studying, analyzing, and determining the factors that lead to successful marriages and those that don't. If we take our own marriages seriously, we should invest time and effort to improve our chances of not only surviving the marriage experience but enjoying it.

We may be surprised to learn from these researchers that conflict in marriage is inevitable and even normal. The idea that a marriage should be free from disagreements is downright unrealistic. Some family counselors blame conflict for marital breakdown, and consequently they recommend couples do damage control.

Much conflict avoidance theory is based on the compatibility concept of married couples. Actually, very few couples are truly compatible. Compatibility is mainly a myth. I advanced the idea in my counseling for decades that the primary objective during courtship is to ascertain whether the two persons are compatible. By that I meant having the same qualities, personality traits, likes, and dislikes. I thought that compatibility would lead to a marriage free of conflict. Today, I have come to a different conclusion.

Dr. William Betcher, a Harvard psychiatrist and psychotherapist, and his coauthor, Robie Ma-cauley, published their findings concerning the causes of marital failure in The Seven Basic Quarrels of Marriage. Concerning conflicts, they conclude:

> These quarrels are necessary because they are rooted in profound
> differences the man and the woman understand only dimly. Only
> by having the quarrel in a new way without destructive tactics
> and with a willingness to learn what lies beneath the surface can
> it ever be solved.[32]

---

32 William Betcher and Robie Macauley, *The Seven Basic Quarrels of Marriage*, pp. 19, 20.

Dr. John Gottman says that when he started his research he felt, as other clinicians did, that too much anger was destructive to a marriage. However, when he investigated the real causes for divorce and separation, he concluded that anger was detrimental to marriages only if it was accompanied by criticism, contempt, defensiveness, and withdrawal.[33] He found that some marriages even fared better if the partners had early disagreements. Later, we will explore these findings and other theories and link them to possible solutions for marriages.

Personal Story

As long as humans have emotions, they will face happy and sad times, excitement and frustration, love and resentment, anger and joy, panic and peace. Precious and I are no different. We had those emotions and more. Unfortunately, with my former wife, it was even more difficult. We didn't have a lot of experience or emotional support from family members to draw on. We got married and lived for most of our married lives in a country away from our relatives. We were on our own. During the struggle to make sense of marriage, we learned and developed homemade techniques to cope with conflict.

It is amazing to me that some people will endure incredible pain and pressures to develop a career, a sport, or a hobby but refuse to struggle with marital issues for the good of the marriage and the spouse he/she claims to "love until death do us part."

Think of the sacrifice of a soldier, the dedication of a mountain climber, the patient endurance of a marathon athlete, the pain inflicted on a football quarterback or running back, or the pu-blic scrutiny and invasion of privacy faced courageously by public figures such as politicians and movie actors/actresses. Many of them quit only when challenged by age, lack of physical strength, or another insuperable factor. They appear to endure it all for the fame, money, and/or power they access. But many of those famous people, as well as the average Joe or Mary, would not tolerate some discomfort at home without engaging in conflicts which often lead to divorce. Rarely do they sincerely seek to discover strategies to deal with the issues which frequently lead to hostility.

Marriage deserves the same effort and patience it takes to train for the Olympic competitions, to become a whiz on the computer, to learn to be a proficient writer, to become a trained electrician, or to be a successful farmer. Nearly everything in life that is worth doing requires the practice of specific strategies and skills for success. The same goes for marriage.

---

33 John Gottman, *Why Marriages Succeed or Fail*, p. 58.

I didn't realize why our marriage survived until I began seriously studying the way marriages work. We had providentially stumbled on a few successful techniques. As we proceed, you will discover some of them.

Pam and I had completely different temperaments. Our differences were the cause of many of our conflicts during our marriage. I have learned that it is difficult to change who I am, namely, my nature. What I did was to discover our differences. With that knowledge, I sought constantly to accommodate my wife's differences, rather than clashing with her. We have learned to be patient with each other even though the differences, though diminished, have not disappeared.

Pam was gracious, patient, and gentle in manner and speech. I am aggressive, impatient, and often loud. Pam has tried to change me over the years with only limited success. For instance, when caught in traffic, I will seek an alternative route immediately. She usually gets annoyed with me for not waiting on the traffic. But I just prefer to keep moving, even if the trip takes longer. Pam dislikes when I speak with a strong voice. She prefers when my voice is subdued, which it rarely is because of my temperament.

Petula and I also have much different characteristics. Having transferred much of my habits to our current relationship, I soon discovered that Precious dislikes much of the same faults in me. Her personality is gentle, calm, slow to act or react and prefers a husband who is just a gentle person. Whom did she marry? An active, creative, visionary, and solution-oriented husband. Often, I speak with a strong voice. I am working on adjusting but changes are painfully slow. Because both of us are challenged by each other's differences, we adjust.

I have found that when disagreements arise between partners, each one frequently claims the high ground of innocence: "It's not my fault". Even if it is clear who is at fault, the guilty spouse will attempt to slither cunningly out of the guilt and consequences.

I developed the approach of ignoring who is at fault and apologizing as soon as my spirit allows. Otherwise, if we each think the fault belongs to our partner, we may wait a long time for the resolution. The problematic process of hurting, blaming, withdrawing, avoiding, reticence, tit-for-tat, unpleasantness, cooling off, warming up, unspoken forgiveness, bonding, and finally back to loving is unpredictable.

This process may be limited to two or more aspects or it may be "the whole nine yards." It may last from a brief period up to a few days. In one instance, with Pam, the process lasted several months because neither of us would relent. What a waste! Somewhere in my marriage I learned to admit the wrong early and initiate a resolution even if I am still hurting. It soon became evident that the pleasure of peace outweighed the pressures of pain caused by the breach in our relationship. Precious reciprocates. One of the best traits Precious has is easily losing grudges. I commend that in her because that is a struggle for me.

Hurt Feelings

Let's explore briefly hurt feelings in relationships. Concerning Pam and me, hurt feelings dominated the cause and duration of conflict. Regardless of the problem between us it was soon forgotten unless one of us was left with hurt feelings. The negative feeling soon takes on a life of its own. It grows imperceptibly, either gradually or suddenly by succeeding words, actions, glances, or even silence. Anything intentional or incidental may trigger an escalation of the perceived wrong.

Let me recount an incident which took place soon after our wedding. We had just arrived in Edmonton, Canada, after our honeymoon in Michigan. We settled into a basement apartment in a quiet neighborhood. A discussion about our past college days came up and Pam wanted to know why I had been so attracted to two of my classmates. I had not concealed my fondness for female friends since I had told Pam at the time that I cherished my freedom to socialize. I pointed out that, although we were friends, we were not married yet. That proved to be a bad decision. I didn't consider the jealousy factor, the insecurity, or the uncertainty my actions generated. One of the girls challenged Pam openly in the girls' dormitory, threatening to take me from her. I was unaware of these events.

Needless to say, I was flabbergasted to learn that these girls used our innocent friendship to undermine my relationship with Pam and that Pam had taken them seriously. She held her feelings from me until after we got married. At that time, I had to face the release of her pent-up emotions. Inexperienced and lacking tact, I responded with impatience. The incident could have escalated into a physical response when emotions flared. It was then that I pledged to myself never to use any physical means to resolve any dispute in our marriage. That decision proved to be lasting.

I recall that my experience of marriage was much different from the five years of close friendship that had preceded it. Before marriage, we met each other at our best; after marriage we had to face each other within four walls. We had to open to each other our range of feelings, attitudes, and manners.

Problems

Some experts may surprise us with research that shows that quarrels are necessary for marriages to succeed. Should we accept this claim? We have lived with the popular view from other experts on family relationships that marital conflict and volatile marriages are destructive, that to live together without ever having a quarrel is the path to happiness. John Gottman, William Betcher, and Robie Macauley have posited the view that conflict in marriage is not critical to the relationship.

The way the issues are resolved and what accompanies the conflict are much more significant.

> Conflict in marriage is not critical to the relationship. Rather, how the issues are resolved and what accompanies the conflict are much more significant.

Significant Signs

Some indications show healthy conflict in a marriage and some important signs indicate that the marriage is heading in the wrong direction.

Normal Conflict

1. Recurring Issues

The seven basic quarrels as Dr. William Betcher outlines them are about gender, loyalties, money, power, children, sex, and privacy. These are recurring themes in marital quarrels. They claim that these are "singled out again and again in therapy practice as the most common, the most emotion filled, and the most deeply rooted of our conflicts."

Most people do not stop to analyze the invisible system that is guiding the marriage. Elements are driving your marriage daily in one direction or another. Most people just go along for the ride. The frightening thing is that some recognize what is taking place when it is too late and too much damage has been done. We shouldn't leave our lives to luck or happenstance. Dr. William Betcher and Robie Macauley say this:

> During early marriage, the discords spring from passion and inexperience; in middle life, there are economic burdens and family obligations; and finally come the disappointments and physical aches of age. The basic quarrel may shift with a new stage of life, or it may arise out of the change. Since people who have been together for a long time tend to assume that they know each other very well, they are surprised when a new basic quarrel materializes in a new season of life.[34]

---

34 William Betcher and Robie Macauley, The Seven Basic Quarrels of Marriage., p. 16.

2. The Secret Formula

Dr. John Gottman developed a magic formula to deal with marital conflict: 5:1 positive to negative equilibrium. As long as five times as many positive interactions and feelings take place between the partners than negative ones, the marriage is likely to succeed.

1. A Successful Strategy

Success is likely when the couple's conflicts lead to:

• Negotiation and compromise;
• Dialogue without hostility;
• Short-lived eruptions of passionate dispute;
• Agreeing to disagree;
• Retaining respect;
• Refraining from extreme expression of anger and frustration.

The marriage is heading for a free fall and collapse if the following are occurring:

• When conflict is accompanied by criticizing, punishing (denying and abusing), controlling, withdrawing, contemptuousness, aggression, ignoring, and defensiveness;
• When one or both partners frequently relate their history negatively. When the marriage is breaking down, they put a negative spin on past experience together;
• When there are frequent hot disputes, accompanied by hurling insults, put-downs, and sarcasm;
• When the partners fail to engage each other, fail to listen;
• When the partners begin to display lack of trust in one another.

Paradigm Three:
Ten Paths to the Pit

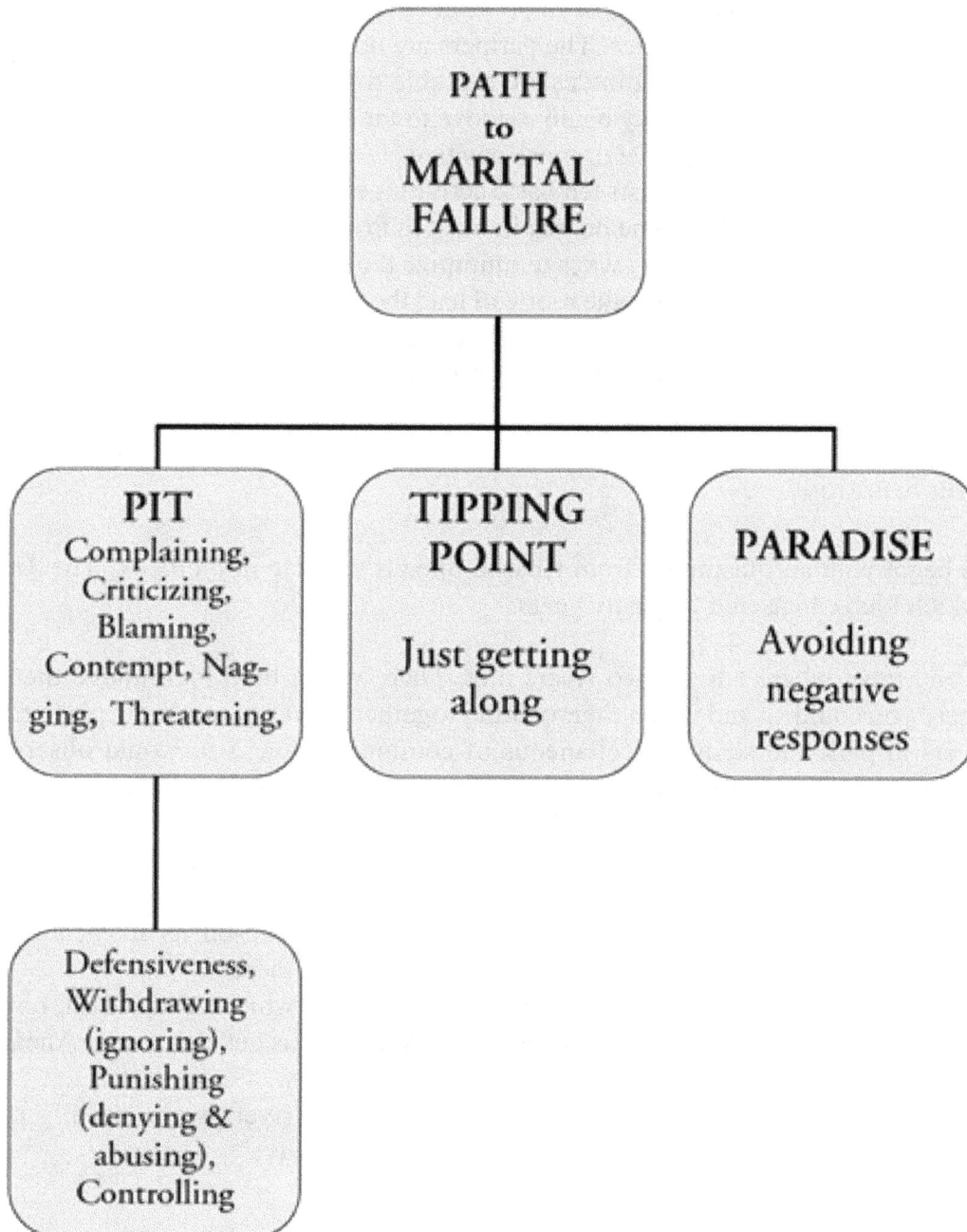

**PATH
to
MARITAL
FAILURE**

PIT
Complaining,
Criticizing,
Blaming,
Contempt, Nag-
ging, Threatening,

**TIPPING
POINT**

Just getting
along

PARADISE

Avoiding
negative
responses

Defensiveness,
Withdrawing
(ignoring),
Punishing
(denying &
abusing),
Controlling

Paradigm Three Explained

Paradigms Three and Four are presented slightly differently. Paradigm Three lists the ten negative influences in marriage, while Paradigm Four lists the ten positive influences. The ten negative attitudes, if practiced, will most likely lead couples down the path to marital failure. The tipping point represents a balance. The partners are not consistently negative but they are not strongly positive either. Their attitudes are bearable for the time being, so they get along. At some point in the future, they may begin to move to the left or right on the chart, especially if one spouse becomes more negative or more positive.

The diagram for Paradigm Three lists ten basic activities which could contribute to the failure of marriage. These are found to some degree in most marriages. What is different for successful marriages is that the partners find ways to minimize the negative effects in the relationship. Allowing these negative attitudes to take root will lead the marriage into the pit. Avoiding these negative responses leaves the way clear for positive attitudes to develop, thereby fostering a spirit of kindness and placing the couple's steps on the path to marital paradise.

Providing Solutions

Let me begin with an illustration from Charlie Shedds's article in the book, The *Marriage Affair*, which I have treasured for many years.

> In one town where I lived two rivers met. There was a bluff high above them where you could sit and watch their coming together. It was a wonderful place for lovers to park and study miscellaneous of communication. You would observe that well upstream, before they united, each river flowed gently along. But right at the point of their union, look out!
>
> Those two nice streams came at each other like fury. I have actually seen them on days when it was almost frightening to watch. They clash in a wild commotion of frenzy and confusion. They hurl themselves head-on as if each was deter-mined that the other should end its existence right there.
>
> Then, as you watched, you could almost see the angry white caps pair off, bow in respect to each other, and join forces as if to say, "Let us get along now. Ahead of us there is something better."
>
> Sure enough, on downstream, at some distance, the river swept steadily on some more. It was broader there, more majestic, and it gave

you the feeling that something good had been fashioned out of the conflict.[35]

This is a metaphor of marriage. Before they meet, the marriage partners are two small gentle flowing streams. At the point of convergence, there is forceful clashing and joining. Afterward, they become like a large peaceful body of water that may serve many purposes.

But first there is the conflict: sorting things out; discovering each other's likes and dislikes; making accommodation for each other's level of comfort. The danger is if that process is aborted or stifled out of some false notion of peace without a price, one or both of the spouses may suppress their personalities to the eventual detriment of the marriage.

Let's see how we may find viable solutions to conflict. Progressive marriage therapists believe that real differences between people can be changed. With proper methods, basic quarrels can be overcome.

> [The greatest barrier to conflict resolution is] rigid thinking—one's conviction either that the spouse is a hopeless case or one can't help reacting intolerantly. People tend to blame their own flawed behavior on circumstances beyond their control and their partner's sins on defects of character.[36]

Dr. William Betcher and Robie Macauley state further:

> One of the most powerful aids that a therapist can bring to any couple who have lost faith in themselves is a new conviction. That conviction says that wounds can be healed, pleasure can return, the marriage can be restored to life. The seven basic quarrels can be overcome.[37]

Acknowledge the Problem

In some relationships only one spouse feels there is a problem. Now that's a real problem. In other cases, the couple just hopes the problem will eventually go away. Some couples don't like to talk about problems. Each partner is afraid to confront the other lest he or she becomes the loser in the conflict that might ensue. Acknowledging that a problem exists is fundamental to the process of

---

35 Charlie Shedd, *The Marriage Affair*, p. 286.
36 William Betcher and Robie Macauley, *The Seven Basic Quarrels of Marriage*, p. 19.
37 William Betcher and Robie Macauley, Ibid., p. 20

seeking a resolution. The approach taken will become a stumbling block or a stepping stone.

Compromise is the method many therapists advocate. But compromise may not be the most popular path couples follow. A study by Dr. Samuel Vuchinich revealed that conflicts ended in compromise only 14 percent of the time. The majority of the time (61 percent, the couple ended the quarrel in a standoff. The spouses maintained their opinions. Twenty-one percent of the time the argument stopped when one conceded and only 4 percent of the time the matter ended with one of the parties walking out of the room.[38] More than compromise is needed to resolve most of the disputes.

> Acknowledging that a problem exists is fundamental to the process of seeking a resolution. The approach taken will become a stumbling block or a stepping stone.

Gender Differences

Both spouses should take into account that they respond to conflict differently. Major cultural and biological differences can limit free communication and understanding. Couples should make every effort to resolve the problem together.

Dr. Gottman has this advice for men:

> Embrace her anger. Do not try to avoid conflict. Sidestepping a problem will not solve it. Rather, it may cause greater problems since your wife may think she is being ignored. Staying and listening to her may be unpleasant, but she is working to keep the marriage healthy. Try to remember that her goal is not to attack you personally, even though it may seem so at times if frustration causes her to couch her complaint in contempt and sarcasm. If you stay with her through this discomfort and listen to her criticisms rather than insisting that she is exaggerating or getting hysterical over nothing, she will calm down. If you stonewall and refuse to listen, she'll be edgy and escalate the conflict, making it more likely that you will end up feeling flooded.[39]

---

38 Samuel Vuchinich, quoted by William Betcher and Robie Macauley, *The Seven Basic Quarrels of Marriage*, p. 274.
39 John Gottman, *Why Marriages Succeed or Fail*, p. 159.

His advice to women:

> Confront him gently. In order to break the vicious cycle of demand/withdrawal, the wife needs to remember that you are emotionally from different planets. Approach him calmly and gently or he may try to withdraw. When you do criticize your husband, remember to tell him you love him and that you just want to change a certain behavior. Try very hard not to slip from complain to criticism and then contempt. He will easily get flooded and then the conflict can quickly escalate. It will be much easier for him to stay engaged if you let him know that talking together about what's bothering you is a way to keep the love between you alive.[40]

The subtitle to book The Seven Basic Quarrels of Marriage is "Recognize, Defuse, Negotiate, and Resolve Your Conflicts."

Many years ago I read a Dagwood and Blondie comic strip that illustrates how a conflict can be avoided. Dagwood is sitting on the steps of his house looking at the bills, obviously discouraged. Observing his downcast appearance, his neighbor comes over and asks him what is wrong. After Dagwood explains, his neighbor berates him and tells him it is his fault he has all those bills because he allows his wife to wrap him around her little finger. He should march inside and set her straight. All this time, without their knowledge, Blondie is overhearing the conversation. As Dagwood enters the door in a huff, Blondie meets him with a charming smile and without saying a word she gives him a smothering kiss, takes him gently by the hand and leads him to his favorite easy chair. She puts his feet up, hands him his favorite pipe and the newspaper, places a pillow behind his head, and commences to massage his feet.

When she finally speaks, she inquires how his day went. Dagwood scratches his head and tries hopelessly to recall the reason he wanted so desperately to talk to his wife. All he seems to recall is the pleasant experience he is having with her.[41]

The biblical Solomon, known as the wise man, counsels us, "A soft answer turns away wrath, but a harsh word stirs up anger." [42]

---

40 John Gottman, Ibid., p. 161.
41 *The Jamaican Sunday Gleaner*, August 1, 1976.
42 Proverbs, Chapter 15:1.

Chapter Four

Control

Preview

The word "control" may spark several ideas in your mind. Some of them might include self-control, controlling another person, controlling something, or being controlled. The marriage relationship encompasses all these meanings, but in marriage the negative impact of control occurs far too frequently and often with devastating results.

I cannot overemphasize the importance of individual freedom. This is a God-given right. Unfortunately, throughout history, some people have sought to dominate others by limiting their freedom. Others surrender their freedom in exchange for something else that appears to be more valuable to them. A person may surrender a portion of his/her freedom to another in exchange for security, safety, or survival. By doing so that person may end up under the other person's control. Resentment, conflict, and dissatisfaction most likely follow, unless the trade-off is very desirable.

In marriage, when control takes hold, it usually does so with an iron grip. It rarely loosens its grip without a struggle. We can be sure of one thing: The controller does not relinquish his control willingly. Sometimes the control ends with great drama.

By its very nature marriage requires that both partners surrender some of their individual rights so that the relationship can thrive. But that should be done within the context of what is best for the success of the marriage or family. Even then, the marriage partners must use wisdom to prevent the surrender of personal responsibility and matters of conscience. Even the rights of children should be guarded. With the exception of very special circumstances, such as serious illness, no adult should surrender control of his/her life to another.

> By its very nature marriage requires that marriage partners surrender some of their individual rights so the relationship can thrive. But that should be done within the context of what is best for the success of the marriage or family. Even then they must use wisdom to prevent the surrender of personal responsibility.

The aim of this chapter is to take a closer look at control in the marriage relationship and how to prevent its negative effects from ruining your marriage and your life.

Personal Story

During our period of friendship, Petula and I had few causes for disagreement. In fact, I can recall only one disagreement of note. As far as we knew, we appeared compatible.

However, soon after our wedding, issues regarding adjustment surfaced. Our freedoms and rights overlapped. Circumstances forced us to react. This was strange for me since during our time of friendship I was accustomed to dealing with Precious only in settings that fostered pleasantries. In reality, we were living in different countries. She lived in Canada and I was in the United States. Suddenly and without any preparation, we were forced to deal with these interpersonal issues requiring immediate resolution.

Because of our personality differences, I assumed a role closer to control. Another factor was that Precious sought my advice for most of her decisions. That caused me to fall back on my background of military training when I had to make quick and firm decisions. I felt it was my responsibility to make most of the decisions. I expected my wife would agree and life would be beautiful. Precious did not like that approach. She preferred collaboration in most areas of our relationship.

At first, my decisiveness was tolerated. Precious assumed certain responsibilities appropriate for women in the family, such as house duties, and I assumed duties appropriate to men, such as providing for the needs of the family. It wasn't long before tensions started to build up and dissatisfaction slowly but surely increased. Fortunately for me, Precious did not pay much attention to many of the women movement's trends. But we could not avoid certain effects of those changes within the society. Today, younger couples take many of these practices for granted. I lived through the changes and Precious certainly experienced some of them. Because we were trained professionally in marriage education, we understood how to adjust quickly. We soon found a reasonable balance.

For instance, because I grew up under the patriarchal pattern of marriage, I did not learn to cook. My cooking skills were limited to porridge and pancakes. My wife despises the former and avoids the latter. She could not cook the meals I liked. We both had to learn together. In matters of sex after marriage, I didn't expect to hear no. With regard to spending money, I expected to have full control. As I mentioned before, Precious was very agreeable and we had very few if any grounds for disagreement at first. Now we had to adjust, and fast.

In my previous relationship, if I decided to follow a particular course of action for the family, I did so single-handedly, leaving little room for dialogue.

With Precious, it is different. She matured gradually into a woman who insisted on her right to make decisions and relied on me only for advice She makes decisions for herself and me. She is graceful but firm. She takes full control of matters pertaining to the house, such as purchasing furniture and arranging them in the house. She would acquire items for the home from time to time. Often, I lose track of where to find simple items in the bathroom or kitchen. I am develping the wisdom to compliment her rather than express my dissatisfaction because I think she is creating unnecessary disruption. I just didn't understand how women function. Now I do!

During one of my marriage motivational presentations, as I explained the way I saw marriage during my twenties, one lady who was attending the session pointed out that my limited view of the role of women was due to my growing up without a mother. My mother passed when I was four years old. But that is not a satisfactory reason since I had a stepmother and during my elementary school years my older sister cared for me and my father. I had plenty of female role models. The truth is that during the fifties and sixties young men were brought up differently than those of later generations.

One day in 1974, Pam and I were driving along Highway 20 in Dorval, Canada, on our way to downtown Montreal. We got into such a heated argument about whether she should buy a new bedroom set that I pulled the car off the highway to discuss the matter with her. Of course, I thought the purchase was unnecessary and I believed I was supposed to have the last word. As the heated discussion continued I got the "Aha." I decided then to relinquish control over certain matters that my wife preferred to handle. Between her upbringing and her instincts, I was no match for her in those areas.

We proceeded calmly to the store to buy a new bedroom set. It served us for many years. That was my first real encounter with my wife's need for independent decision making in our marriage. There were many other painful lessons for me to learn about control. I practice those lessons learned in our current home.

During the first few years of our marriage, Precious and I shopped together for everything. Most of our decisions were made together. I resisted it at first because I was not accustomed to the places she shopped, choices she made, and her questions about what to buy. She resented my responses but I learned to accommodate her.

Eventually, after learning her purchasing habits, I can go shopping with her. Our choices are often similar. In addition, I congratulate Precious for shopping wisely. Before understanding her, she would insist that I go shopping with her. Now, we have a great arrangement that works for both of us.

All this time I felt as though I was losing control. Our relationship was growing but I became more and more negative about Precious' choices. She was maturing into a wise woman and wife. I didn't understand her. But now I do. It took years for me to mature and realize that my wife is entitled to her own decisions provided they do not jeopardize our important plans and goals.

Problem

Dominance

In North America, our modern view of marriage is rooted in biblical traditions. However, a very strong movement to break from the biblical foundation of marriage is currently gaining hold in our society. There are those who still prefer to preserve its spiritual as well as traditional underpinnings. However, it is difficult to rely on society's interpretation of the biblical position regarding marriage since religious leaders in the past have used different interpretations of the same scripture to affirm different positions on the roles of husband and wife. In the American society for instance, the Bible has been used to support men's dominance over women. Yet others use it to liberate women through freedom of choice and spiritual gifts, which are equally correct biblical teachings.

Even in today's society, some churches struggle to keep women from being ordained as members of the clergy. Those against ordaining women claim that the Bible teaches that women are to be followers, not leaders. While there may be good arguments on both sides, in all honesty we should not conclude that God ordained the subservience of women. The same Bible is replete with examples of women functioning in leadership positions.

For thousands of years men have followed the practice of dominating women in society. But that does not make the practice right. Throughout much of recorded history, nations have attacked their neighbors or perpetrated slavery. Who seeks to defend these brutal practices? God has placed in every human heart the desire to be free. I am amazed it took millennia for women to gain their freedom, at least in western societies. That same spirit of freedom should be experienced in every marriage and every family.

Every successful business and progressive country has some type of organization. Consider any sport. How successful would the game of baseball be if all the members of the team were excellent pitchers and poor batters? Or, how successful would a football team become if everyone trained to be quarterbacks and none trained to play defense? Likewise in a marriage, the creator in his wisdom assigned roles to each spouse for the smooth running of the home and ultimately for each partner's happiness. Men have a role and so do women. It is certain, however, their functions do not require dominance or control over each other. Nature has dictated to a great extent the roles to which each is best suited.

Husband and wife should support each other as a team rather than oppose each other as competitors.

> The roles of marriage partners do not require dominance or control. Nature has dictated to a great extent the roles to which each is best suited. Husband and wife should support each other as a team rather than oppose each other as competitors.

Anger and Aggression

Men use aggression to control women. Women are more likely to use aggression as a defense mechanism or to retaliate. Researchers have studied the behavior of males and females to determine the reason they act so differently. You guessed it: The researchers came to different conclusions. We need to consider the differences in the behavior of the sexes because they provide clues to the reason for male/female conflict. If knowledge is power, then a better understanding of these differences may help us avoid these types of marital problems.

> Men use aggression to control women. Women are more likely to use aggression as a defense mechanism or to retaliate.

Dr. Neil Boyd, a professor of criminology, studied the differences in behavior of males and females. Why do most boys love to engage in rough sports and play while most girls prefer to play with dolls and kitchen toys? His research led him to the conclusion that the origin of sexually oriented behavior is in the genes. Other academics say the difference is due to socialization. They think that boys are taught to be physically forceful and girls are trained to be quiet and cooperative.

Researcher Diane McGuinness and her students watched thirty-eight boys and thirty-eight girls, ages three to five, play without supervision in their pre-school. Girls participated in half as many physical activities as boys did. Boys were more likely to hit another child and to use a toy for a purpose other than that for which it was designed.[43]

When a dispute arose for instance, whether the person was "out" or not in a game of tag the boys would argue and find a way to continue the game. The girls engaged in a similar dispute would end the game and go home. The likely conclusion is that boys love aggression and com-petition so much that they prefer

---

43 See: Neil Boyd, *The Beast Within*, p. 60.

to find a way to continue. Girls, less inclined to value competition and fearful of damaging friendly relationships, avoid the conflict by ending the game.[44]

Psychologist and criminologist Dr. Anne Campbell and other researchers conclude that even though differences begin in biology, environment plays a vital role in shaping the differences in the behavior of the sexes. Dr. Anne Campbell states:

> Whereas a boy moves away from his mother's condemnatory, expressive view of aggression into a world of men, where its instrumental value is understood, the girl makes no such change. She remains selec- tively tuned into a female wavelength, searching for clues to femininity and to aggression…. The most remarkable thing about the socializa- tion of aggression in girls is its absent.[45]

Whereas men use aggression to dominate, women tend to suppress it. There are two schools of thought concerning aggression: expressive and instrumental.

Expressive aggression:

> In an expressive representation, anger is tinged with fear. It feels like a rising crescendo of imminent chaos culminating in an abandonment of reason and control.[46]

Instrumental aggression:

> This type uses aggression to humiliate, control, and conquer.

How does this information affect marriages? Rightly understood, it is crucial in the reaction of spouses to each other. First, we need to be aware that women are more likely to use expres- sive aggression and men are more likely to use instrumental aggression. Second, men and women interpret aggression differently. As a result, since couples use and interpret aggression differently, it may lead to greater stresses within the marriage. Often, they are not aware that the root of the problem is in their biology, their gender differences. Dr. Anne Campbell says: "[F] or women aggression is the failure of self-control, while for men it is the imposing of control over others."[47]

---

44 William Betcher, *The Seven Quarrels of Marriage*, p. 139.
45 Anne Campbell, *Men, Women, and Aggression*, p. 20.
46 Anne Campbell, Ibid., p. 15.
47 Campbell, Ibid., p. 1.

Men are more likely to use aggression without anger. Women use it as a signal of emotional upset. Men use aggression to instill fear and gain control over another person. Men move more quickly from verbal abuse to physical aggression. That explains the reason men consider the way women express anger and aggression to be senseless since it does little to gain power and control. When some women are upset, they want to talk it through, be left alone, or cry. Men prefer to act. Men see crying as a strategy women use to gain control. That's misunderstanding women, since they cry to discharge tension and frustration. Women's approach is victimless.

> Men often consider the way women express anger and aggression senseless since it does little to gain power and control. When some women are upset, they want to talk it through, be left alone, or cry. Men prefer to act.

The Passive-Aggressive Person

Men are more likely to engage in passive-aggressive behaviors. They use this method in the work-place and more destructively at home. The passive-aggressive behavior is an attempt by someone who lacks empowerment to challenge the threat indirectly and covertly. Scott Wetzer, who wrote a book on the subject, says passive- aggressive behavior occurs "[when] the passive-aggressive man misconstrues personal relationships as being struggles for power, and sees himself as powerless."[48]

The passive-aggressive man will deny women their feelings and needs, close off opportunities to resolve problems, and focus on how he can get his own way. He draws you in and then lets you down. He tells a woman he can't live without her but he can't commit for the long term. He leaves her with the feeling that she did something to hurt him. The passive-aggressive man will seek to control you by "tapping the weak spot in your willpower, [exploiting] any hesitation on your part, and will constantly challenge your resolve."[49]

---

48 Scott Wetzer, *Living With the Passive-aggressive Man.*, p. 15.
49 Scott Wetzer, Ibid., p. 52.

Sex and Control

Two paragraphs in the book Making Marriage Meaningful may explain adequately the complex issue of using sex to control one's partner.

Using sex to control one's partner is a double-edged sword. It may succeed in drawing the necessary attention to the present concern of the aggrieved spouse, but hurt feelings caused by rejection will most likely result in retaliation. Both husband and wife may be guilty of using sex in their quest for control. It may help a spouse assert a position of power over the other person, but it will likely result in resentment. Despite the assertion of women's autonomy in today's society, many men still feel they are in control. When it comes to marriage, however, they find that to gain a successful relationship, they need to exchange their dominance for emotional equality. By so doing, they make themselves vulnerable. In the hands of untrustworthy wives, they may be humiliated. Men are concerned that their wives may interpret their surrender to intimacy to be a sign of weakness. Some women do.

Abusive husbands, who may feel threatened by their vulnerability, retreat and resort to verbal and physical abuse in their quest to regain control. They feel that intimacy allows women to gain control. If they think they are losing control and the women assert control, even tempolarity in the case of withholding sex, they may abandon their feeling of closeness and loving concern for the familiar feeling of power, competition, and control. Consequently, they will no longer feel powerless and at the mercy of their wives. Here lies a fertile ground for serious misinterpretation of the spouses' feelings, actions, and intent. By with- holding sex, women may be signaling their need for intimacy or a demonstration of affection prior to sex. Men may interpret that as rejection and thereby seek to retaliate.[50]

> In order for both partners to have satisfying sex and a successful marital relationship, they must surrender their effort to control and replace it with the desire for a shared experience.

Some power struggles may be displayed in the bedroom in overt or covert forms. Still other effects may be more subtle. The psychological effect of loss of control may result in uncontrolled lower level of sexual performance. Impotence or premature ejaculation in men and frigidity in women may be temporary conditions caused by loss of

50 Robert Samms, Making Marriage Meaningful, p. 52.

control may result in uncontrolled lower level of sexual performance. Impotence or premature ejaculation in men and frigidity in women may be temporary conditions caused by loss of-control. In order for both partners to have satisfying sex and a successful marital relationship, they must surrender their effort to control and replace it with the desire for a shared experience.

Paradigm Four:
Ten Paths to Paradise

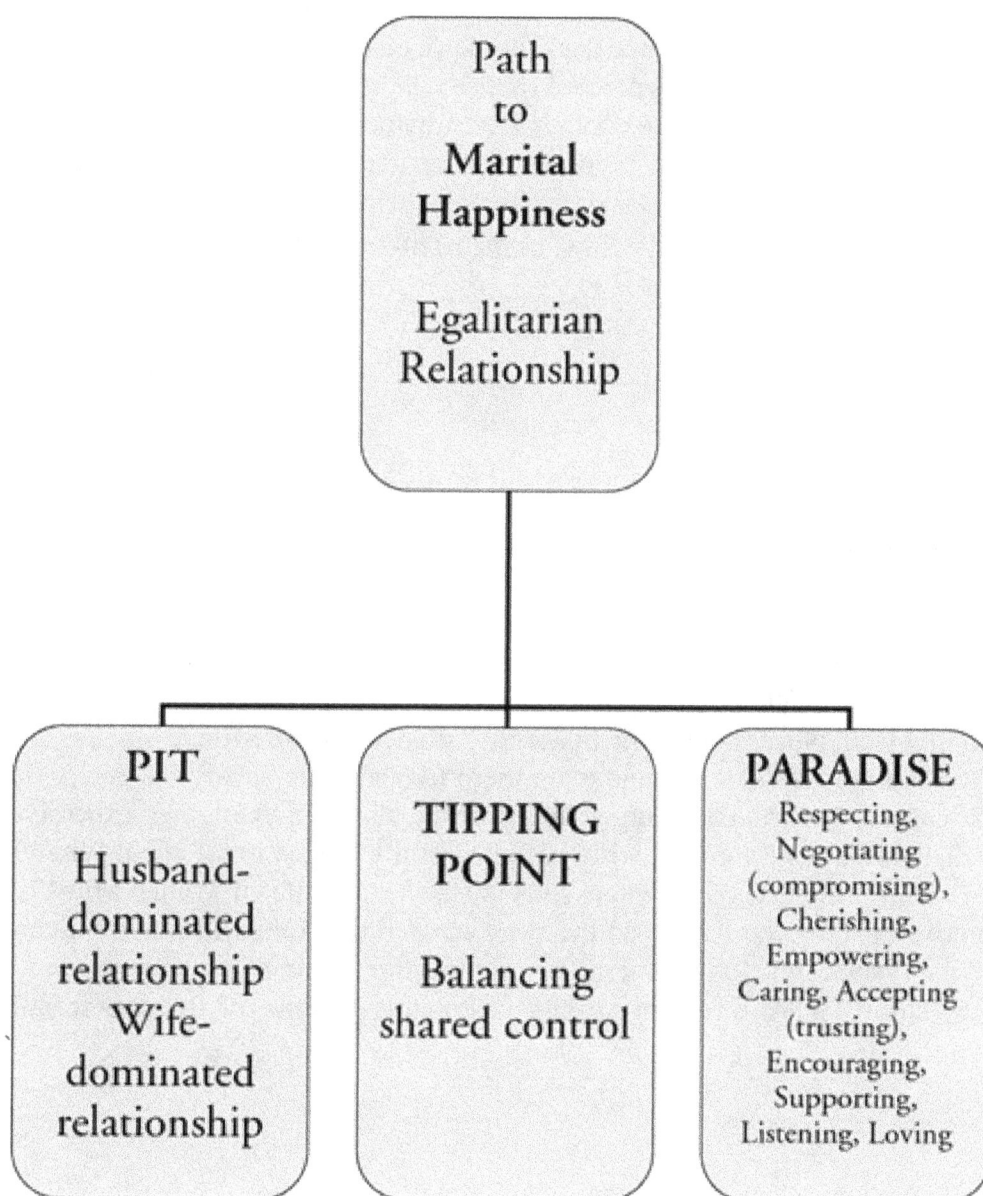

Path
to
Marital
Happiness

Egalitarian
Relationship

PIT

Husband-
dominated
relationship
Wife-
dominated
relationship

TIPPING
POINT

Balancing
shared control

PARADISE
Respecting,
Negotiating
(compromising),
Cherishing,
Empowering,
Caring, Accepting
(trusting),
Encouraging,
Supporting,
Listening, Loving

Paradigm Four Explained

In the previous chapter we focused on the negative elements which, if allowed to fester in the marriage, will lead to pain and problems. Paradigm Four provides a contrast. These ten attributes, when fostered in the marriage relationship, will result in positive responses from marriage partners, thereby leading to marital success.

Wife-dominated/husband-dominated relationships occur when either the wife or the husband exerts strong control over the other and seeks to perpetuate it. Whenever that occurs in a marriage there is a real danger that the oppressed spouse will be dissatisfied and will eventually withdraw his/her support. As long as the control is less than oppressive, the couple will get along, but they may remain near the tipping point. As dissatisfaction occurs, they will drift toward the pit. As the relationship becomes a shared experience, the couple will move toward paradise.

Ten ways to achieve paradise are specified in the right-hand column of the diagram above.

Providing Solutions

Egalitarian (Shared Relationship

When either the husband or wife dominates, the relationship approach may at first appear to be successful. However, it most likely will lead to conflict as the oppressed spouse matures in the relationship and desires freedom to function within the marriage.

I observed one couple who appeared to be happily married. The wife was extremely dominant. The husband was constantly responsive to her. From all appearances they were happily married and functioning well. Nevertheless, the husband, forbidden by his wife to smoke, hid his cigarettes in the shed behind the house and went there frequently to satisfy his desire. Just before he died of cancer, he had the courage to confront his wife about her excessive control. Later, she discovered his cigarettes, which were carefully hidden in the shed. When I think of this couple, I am reminded of the short story "The Secret Life of Walter Mitty," by James Grover Thurber. Those who have read the story or seen the film will readily understand the impact of dominance within the marriage relationship. Walter Mitty developed a coping shadow persona-lity. When he escaped to that personality, he enjoyed freedom from his wife's control.

The better choice is an egalitarian (equal relationship because it gives each partner the opportunity to express his/her views and desires, unfettered by the spouse's control. It fosters tolerance and understanding, which are key ingredients in a successful relationship.

The control one spouse exerts over another is effective primarily when that spouse gains a position of power over the other. The dominance of the wife (wife-dominant relationship) or the dominance of the husband (husband-dominant relationship) is a strong form of control. Ge-nerally, the one who has the upper hand in setting the rules has the control. The quarrels about control can be bitter ones since both partners want the immediate and long-term advantage. In these relationships, control May shift back and forth depending on whose tactics are winning at the time.

> Generally, the one who has the upper hand in setting the rules has the control. The quarrels about control can be bitter ones since both want the immediate and long-term advantage.

The more enduring approach, which is harder to achieve, is the egalitarian relationship. Both spouses share control and decision-making. Some of the tactics or strategies couples use frequently are listed below.

> The more enduring approach, which is harder to achieve, is the egalitarian relationship. Both spouses share control and the decision-making.

Tactics by the Weaker Spouse

- Controlling: dropping hints, flattering, seducing, reminding the spouse of past favors, bribing.
- Indirection: pleading, crying, pretending to be ill, and acting helpless.
- Withdrawing: sulking, generating guilt, playing the martyr, walking away.

Tactics by the Stronger Spouse

- Aggression: threatening, insulting, ridiculing, and becoming violent.
- Dominating: claiming to be more informed, asserting authority, suppressing the others' views.

Strategies by Egalitarian Spouses

- Negotiating: listening, reasoning, compromising, offering trade-offs, surrendering, sharing.

Married couples must first confront their need for sharing power and control. Some marriage partners don't even want to talk about it since they are fearful that they will lose their spouse's support. Some married partners fear that discussing their dissatisfaction may incur the wrath of their spouse and lead to more unpleasantness. However, in order for changes to occur, the couple must seek and obtain a reasonable level of freedom in the relationship. Suffering in silence will only lead to unhappiness with the marriage.

A Personal Note

Fortunately for me, I discovered early in my marriage that my assumptions about power and control were not workable in the long term. Precious was ready to assert her control. She was calm and graceful but firm. It was like a baby who is ready to be born. It was not that Precious did not see the need for exerting control earlier; rather, I was insensitive to her desire to exert control and she was graceful not to be too assertive. I just didn't think about Precious' need for control.

Unfortunately, I did not change overnight. I have a built-in desire to be confrontational and decisive. I am still learning to slow down and use more diplomacy in decision-making with Precious and my children. Precious is naturally calm and patient, yet she is also determined. She knows what she wants or prefers to do and she acts strategically and diplomatically, yet irresistibly. She is usually shaken by my approach and I am usually impatient with hers. I recognized the problem early in our marriage but I did not seek to solve it until it started to affect our relationship directly. My conscious decision to share power and control with Precious contributed to our marital survival.

Choose Your Battles

A secret weapon Precious uses throughout our marriage is to allow me to make my own decisions in matters important to me while she controls what she considers important to her. It's in harmony with one of my leadership philosophies: Pick your battles. Make sure you pick the ones you can win.

> A secret weapon Precious uses throughout our marriage is to allow me to make my own decisions in matters important to me while she controls what she considers important to her.

Have you ever been in a class or on a committee with people who had something to say on every subject or issue? They don't even take time to think. They talk, talk, and talk. Usually, those are the ones who make average or below average grades or are least effective in persuading others in the group. When you choose your issues and plan your approach, you are much more effective. Sometimes you have to let other important issues or points go. In order to be effective when you present your issue, you need to await your opportunity. Doing so will help preserve your credibility and effectiveness when you need to win or achieve your advantage? So it is with marriage. Trying to correct, instruct, and direct your spouse constantly become control by nagging. After a time he/she tunes you out or seeks refuge in other less acceptable ways. These may include "silent submission, ineffective fighting, blaming, and emotional distancing."[51]

Dealing with Anger

Dr. Harriet Lerner wrote The Dance of Anger to help women deal with anger. Men can benefit from it both for themselves and to gain a better understanding of their wives. She makes this point:

> We cannot make another person change his or her steps to an old
> dance, but if we change our steps, the dance no longer can continue
> in the same predictable pattern.[52]

To make changes, we need to STOP and consider our own part in the conflict that leads us to become angry. No one can really make you angry. That's something you do. It is not something someone makes you do. I was surprised when I read Dr. William Glasser's comment that some people choose to depress. I always thought that depression was externally or internally imposed on an individual because of too much stress. As a reputable psychiatrist, he knows about depression. He insists that people choose many things about their lives and depression and anger are among them. Dr. Lerner makes the point in another way:

---

51 Harriet Lerner, *The Dance of Anger*, p. 10.
52 Harriett Lerner, *The Dance of Anger*, p. 14.

Even rats in a maze learn to vary their behavior if they keep hitting a dead end. Why in the world, then, do we behave less intelligently than laboratory animals? [53]

The answer may be fear or passivity. Most people prefer to remain with what is familiar. The threat of having to reorganize one's life's pattern and habits cause some people to recoil and remain with the problem because it is familiar territory. However, if your life is to improve, you must face the unfamiliar from time to time.

> To make changes, we need to STOP and consider our own part in the conflict that leads us to become angry. No one can really make you angry. That's something you do. It is not something someone makes you do.

When seeking to improve your relationship, you cannot use a "hit and run" approach. You must reflect on the causes of your anger and frustration and study effective ways to bring about change. After pointing out that we must tune into the sources of our anger and clarify where we stand, Dr. Lerner suggests that we ask ourselves specific questions:

- What about this situation that caused me to be angry?
- What is the real issue involved?
- What do I think and feel?
- Who is really responsible?
- What do I want to change?
- What am I willing to do and what am I not willing to do?

The questions look simple but they can be challenging when tackled seriously with the view of bringing about permanent changes in our lives. Dr. Lerner writes:

It is amazing how frequently we march off to battle without knowing what the war is all about. We may be putting our anger energy into trying to change or control a person who does not want to change, rather than putting that same energy into getting clear about our own position and choices. This is especially true in our closest relationships,

---

53 Harriett Lerner, Ibid., p. 44.

where, if we do not learn to use our anger first to clarify our own thoughts, feelings, priorities, and choices, we can easily get trapped in endless cycles of fighting and blaming that go nowhere. Managing anger effectively goes hand in hand with developing a clearer "I" and becoming a better expert on the self.[54]

The Strategy of Surrendering

When I saw the book The Surrendered Wife, my reaction was that it was the sentimental expressions of a submissive woman, perhaps out of the early twentieth century ethos. When I gave it to Pam for her feedback, after glancing at it, her opinion was similar to mine. This is, of course, before we read the book. The title left me with the impression that Laura Doyle had given up her rights in the marriage and allowed her husband to control her. I could not have been more wrong. When a closer look revealed that it was a twenty-first century publication, Laura Doyle got my attention. I learned much from her journey of moving from a frustrated wife to a happy spouse and so can you.

At age twenty-two, Laura married John and enjoyed a blissful marriage at first. Here is the gist of what happened next.

Then, I started to see John's imperfections more glaringly, and I began correcting him. It was my way of helping him improve. From my point of view, if he would just be more ambitious at work, more romantic at home, and clean up after himself, everything would be fine. I told him as much.

He didn't respond well. And it's no wonder. What I was really trying to do was control John. The harder I pushed, the more he resisted, and we both grew irritable and frustrated. While my intentions were good, I was clearly on the road to marital hell. In no time I was exhausted from trying to run my life and his. Even worse, I was becoming estranged from the man who had once made me so happy. Our marriage was in serious trouble and it had only been four years since we'd taken our vows.[55]

Laura's loneliness increased the more she tried to control John. She became desperate in her search for the answer to her marital deadlock. Laura's search led her through therapy, reading books on marriage, and talking to other women

---

54 Harriett Lerner, Ibid., p. 13.
55 Laura Doyle, *The Surrendered Wife*, pp. 13, 14.

about their successful experiences. During this journey, Laura discovered a few vital keys to marital happiness: surrendering to the marriage, developing trust in her spouse, and practicing freedom from external controls.

After following the process that transformed her marriage, Laura remarked:

> Today I call myself a surrendered wife because when I stopped trying to control the way John did everything and started trusting him implicitly, I began to have the marriage I've always dreamed of.[56]

The change didn't occur overnight. It's not a hit and run affair. It is a total change of attitude, which will involve you in a crucial struggle. Then, it becomes easier and easier until you reach your goal. That's how it happened for Pam and me and that's how Laura described her path to success as well. I discovered that surrender did not mean giving up; rather, it meant transitioning from external controls to self-control. It meant giving up the futile effort of trying to change someone else, who may not even desire to change, to exercise your freedom of choice to change your attitude and paddle your own canoe to the happiness you desire.

> Surrender means giving up the futile effort of trying to change someone else, who may not even desire to change, to exercise your freedom of choice to change your attitude and paddle your own canoe to the happiness you desire.

Laura shares her intimate results with us. She reports:

> As I stopped bossing him around, giving him advice, burying him in lists of chores to do, criticizing his ideas and taking over every situation as if he couldn't handle it, something magical happened. The union I dreamed of appeared.
> The Man who wooed me was back. We were intimate again. Instead of keeping a running list of complaints about how childish and irresponsible he was, I felt genuine gratitude and affection for John. We were sharing our responsibilities without blame or resentment. Instead of bickering all the time, we were laughing together, holding hands, dancing in the kitchen, and enjoying an electrifying closeness that we hadn't had for years.[57]

---

56 Laura Doyle, *The Surrendered Wife*, p. 14.
57 Laura Doyle, Ibid., p. 18.

By the way, I have always thought that happiness and peace come from within, not from external sources. I do not expect happiness to come from my spouse, a car, a house, or money in the bank. They make my life more pleasant but my real sense of well-being comes from within. I really mean that.

Chapter Five

Compromise

Preview

When we hear that a couple is having ongoing conflict, we usually consider the remedy to be communication and/or compromise. Especially if the troubled spouses are relatives or friends, we expect that if they talk to each other more or give in to each other, they will be able to resolve their conflict. However, the solution may not be that straightforward.

To communicate effectively requires more than just talking to each other. To compromise in order to bring about harmony in a troubled marriage may also be very difficult to achieve. Compromise should be the result of a process that ought to precede it. The process is called negotiation. Negotiation will be enhanced when the spouses first try to determine the reasons for the conflict or disagreement. As in our marriage, some couples struggle for years with disagreement after disagreement without knowing the root cause. Some couples learn to live with the recurring problems; others, after suffering enough pain, give up the marriage. Our goal at this point is to consider the concepts and strategies that produce effective compromise.

> Compromise should be the result of a process that ought to precede it. The process is called negotiation.

Personal Story

When Precious and I got married, the early blush of love and novelty kept us from taking note of each other's differences. As we got more in touch with each other on a day to day basis, the differences began to matter. Accommodation did not occur automatically. In fact, I believe that for most of our marriage compromising each other's differences rather than dealing directly with them was more likely the path we followed.

It was not until a few years into our marriage that we figured out that some things had to be dealt with and resolved. By that time Precious and I were getting weary of these recurring issues anyway.

Even though I loved my wife, my idea of marriage was to win my wife over to my point of view. As she matured in the relationship, however, she gradually desired to assert her influence into the decision-making process. She never surrendered her calm, graceful manner, but she was strong and determined. Our wills began to clash. Instead of relenting, I resisted compromise.

Our differences ranged from dealing with the children to the purchasing of household items to disagreement over the level of my voice when addressing her. We didn't have conflicts over the big issues like money, where to live, or lack of trust. But the small things were unwelcome irritants nevertheless.

For my 1985 New Year's resolution, I decided to change my attitude to my former wife and thereby create a more pleasant home for our children. I was miserable by that time anyway, and I suppose my wife and children were not enjoying our relationship. The decision that changed my attitude one hundred and eighty degrees was this: I decided to consider only my part in any misunderstanding. That meant that whenever a problem developed between us, I would consider only the contribution I could make to resolve it. Prior to that time, I was always concerned about what Pam was doing wrong and how she was hurting my feelings. I no longer focused on her. This was the beginning of a long struggle to deal with problems and misunderstandings between us. But we were on the road to success. I did not feel I was abandoning any principles in order to compromise, rather I believed I was making an effort to accommodate my wife's opinions. I certainly needed to be more sensitive to her feelings and desires.

If you had paid close attention to my approach to resolving our marital problems, you would have observed that even though we made progress toward resolving the conflicts, something was missing in the process. Negotiation!

Problem

Some people's concept of compromise is giving up your rights to another person in order to achieve peace and avoid conflict. When that occurs in a marriage without the other partner acknowledging his/her part in what has occurred, abuse of the innocent spouse could occur with devastating results. Let's say the husband dominates the wife and children. In the process, he limits their freedom and opportunity to develop a sense of well-being and self-worth. In addition, he blames his wife whenever anything goes wrong in the home. If the wife were to give up more of her rights to pacify her husband, she would be contributing to her own abuse. Both spouses need to consider the root causes of the problem before proceeding to attempt long-term solutions.

> If the wife were to give up more of her rights to pacify her husband, she would be contributing to her own abuse. Both spouses need to consider the root causes of the problem before proceeding to attempt long-term solutions.

Need-Strength Profile

Dr. William Glasser, whom Pastor Robert Schuller called "the world's greatest psychiatrist," developed the concept of the Need-Strength Profile. He believes that the genetic basis of our personality determines to a great extent how we think, function, and live our lives. Often, we see these traits in people and consider them characteristic of that person. As Dr. William Glasser explains, we think of someone as fun loving, a compulsive spender, a risk taker, an independent thinker, or use similar descriptive tags to identify them. While he admits that it is difficult to separate those traits which are acquired through heredity from those learned from the environment, he believes that five basic traits are genetically determined: survival, love and belonging, power, freedom, and fun.

Dr. Glasser used these five traits to develop what he called a Need-Strength Profile. This is a reliable tool to determine the compatibility of the partners before or during marriage. For a couple to match their level of strength or weakness on each of these traits, both partners must bring to a conscious level the reasons they would agree or disagree on issues related to these traits.

> Once the partners determine their level of strength or weakness based on these traits and compare them with each other, they will begin to understand the reason they are having problems in those areas in which they have significant differences.

Needs from Nature and Nurture

As I did further research and contemplated this concept regarding the true basis of our needs, I was led in a different direction from Dr. Glasser's conclusion. I felt that couples could benefit even more from this approach if they considered Dr. Glasser's five basic needs of nature and those acquired from nurture. There are basic characteristics which they acquired both from their heredity as well as from their environment. I have identified ten traits, including those identified by William Glasser. They are:

> Power, Freedom, Creativity (progress), Security, Fun,
> Love (companionship & belonging), Survival, Self-esteem,
> Comfort (peace), and Recognition.

Once the partners determine their level of strength or weakness based on these traits and compare them with those of their spouse, they will begin to understand the reason they are having problems in those areas in which they have significant differences.

The Compatibility Myth

During the past several decades many marriage professionals have believed that compatibility holds the key to marital success. A marriage matchmaking company, which frequently advertises on television and radio, says that its success in matching couples is based on compatibility. The goal of this company is to find people with similar traits and match them together for the perfect marriage.

However, as noble as that goal may appear to be, we must take into consideration that people change over time. Maturity, pressures from societal forces, influence of family and friends, exposure to certain ideas, dormant earlier experiences, and a myriad of other elements affect people over time, sometimes to significant degrees. Compatibility or finding one's soul mate may seem like a desirable goal but several contrary forces could easily derail what seemed like peace and tranquility and the "happy ever after" prospective future for many unsuspecting couples.

For much of the previous three decades before I embarked upon this marriage motivational series, I gave each engaged couple preparing for marriage a professional compatibility marriage prediction profile on which to base my counseling. It revealed the strengths and weaknesses in that developing relationship. When I point out my findings, the couple may choose to go forward with the wedding, delay the wedding, or even break off the relationship.

Of all the couples I dealt with, one couple stood out in this regard. The couple received nearly a perfect score on the compatibility test. Following the wedding, they lived happily together for a while and had one child. Few years later, I discovered to my amazement that they had a bitter divorce after only a few years of marriage. The main reason for their divorce was in one of the areas of compatibility where they scored highest. Their marriage began to unravel when the husband became disillusioned about a previously satisfying religious faith and the other spouse chose to remain firm in her faith. Their values and common interests began to change rapidly until lack of support for each other led to hostility.

When I counseled youth during my formative years in my profession, I emphasized the importance of compatibility. I believed that two young people who are attracted to each other should determine whether they are compatible before deciding to get married. Today, my emphasis is different. I am alerted to the fact that no two people are really compatible. They may share similar character traits or have similar beliefs and values but they are different personalities and will experience life differently regardless of how compatible they may appear. A closer look may detect those differences, or time may be needed to reveal them. Granted that some couples are closer to each other than others, but the differences are there nonetheless. In addition, people change constantly as they mature and expand their knowledge and experience. Couples should be prepared to face those eventualities as well.

Paradigm Five:
Ten Needs of Nature & Nurture

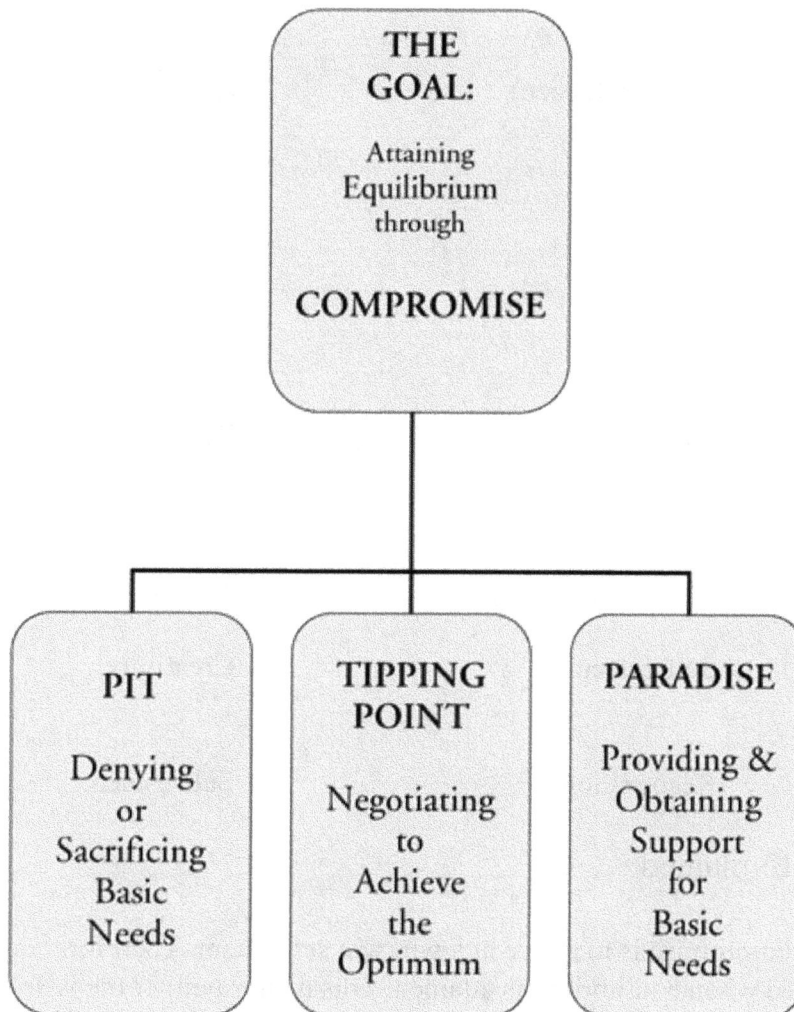

THE GOAL:

Attaining
Equilibrium
through

COMPROMISE

PIT

Denying
or
Sacrificing
Basic
Needs

TIPPING POINT

Negotiating
to
Achieve
the
Optimum

PARADISE

Providing &
Obtaining
Support
for
Basic
Needs

Needs of Nature & Nurture

Husband	Wife
Freedom	Love (belonging)
Love (companionship)	Security
Power	Survival
Comfort (peace)	Comfort (peace)
Creativity	Fun
Security	Power (influence)
Fun	Recognition
Survival	Freedom
Self-esteem	Creativity
Recognition	Self-esteem

Paradigm Five Explained

A main goal of compromise is to arrive at a win/win settlement. Therefore, in marriage, compromise is achieved when equilibrium is attained. This means neither the wife nor the husband is surrendering more than they can afford in order to remain happy in the marriage. When that principle is breached, one or both spouses may be dissatisfied or become miserable. If they sacrifice too much to gain a compromise, the marriage may head toward the pit. On the other hand, if the partners find a way to satisfy each other's basic needs without sacrificing their own, the marriage is growing toward paradise.

Couples should be aware of each spouse's level of need in each of these areas and be prepared to make the necessary adjustments for each other's comfort and well-being. In so doing, the marriage will benefit.

All people have needs. Some arise from their genes, those with which they are endowed by their parents (nature), and other needs arise from those acquired by their environment (nurture). We function day by day and are happy or unhappy according to the denial or satisfaction derived from these needs. Basically, these needs determine to a large extent who we are. Each person, therefore, functions daily with the level of response to his/her needs. Let's say that John and Mary get married. John is fun loving, enjoys his freedom, and doesn't care much for his sur- vival, i.e., he takes risks and doesn't care for his health. Mary enjoys being at home, doesn't like going out for entertainment, is concerned about her health, and loves the security of being with her husband.

Soon after the honeymoon period passes, they will have to face the reality of their differences. If they take the approach of one sacrificing his/her needs for the other, unhappiness will most likely occur.

The model of Paradigm Five requires that both the partners acknowledge their differences and negotiate them rather than going directly into compromise. The goal is to search for the optimum level of satisfaction through negotiation and compromise. While the process is occurring and they are neither satisfied nor dissatisfied, they are said to be at the tipping point. As they fail to meet each other's needs, they begin to move toward the pit. As they begin to satisfy each other's needs, they move toward paradise.

> Marriage is creating a partnership, which builds up a reservoir of emotional support.

Providing Solutions

The main reason two people get married is to enhance their happiness by giving constant support and emotional nurturance to each other. When disagreements erupt, the free flow of their harmony, pleasure, and happiness take flight. Every effort should be made to resolve problems as soon as possible. The Bible counsels:

> Be angry but do not sin; do not let the sun go down on your
> anger....Let all bitterness and wrath and anger and clamour
> and slander

be put away from you, with all malice, and be
kind to one another, tenderhearted, forgiving one another,
as God in Christ forgave you.[58]

The authors of *The Good Marriage* pointed out that:

Our needs for comforting and encouragement are deep and lasting.
A main task of every marriage from the early days of the relationship
to its end is for each partner to nurture the other.[59]

Marriage creates a partnership, which builds up a reservoir of emotional support. When called upon this reservoir has the capacity "to give comfort and encouragement in a relationship that is safe for dependency, failure, disappointment, mourning, illness, and aging in short, for being a vulnerable human being."[60]

The 50/50 Marriage Myth

In the marriage experience, couples need to determine whether they really want the maximum from the relationship or they should strive for the optimum. To attempt to get your spouse to give equally in everything as you do is courting disaster. People have different strengths and weaknesses. Successful couples discover the best ways to accentuate each other's strengths and avoid emphasizing their weaknesses. In effect, they give support to each other's areas of weakness.

> To attempt to get your spouse to give equally in everything as you do is courting disaster.

Laura Doyle,[61] who questioned whether her marriage was worth keeping, saved her marriage after abandoning her unrealistic expectation of sharing responsibilities equally. She realized that the relationship with her husband would be enhanced if she functioned on her husband's strengths rather than his weaknesses. She opted for equilibrium through compromise. Rather than pressing her husband to fulfill her maximum expectation, she settled for an optimum level of performance from him. (Optimum is a balanced level of satisfaction for both partners as opposed to the highest level of satisfaction.) The responsibilities are shared, not necessarily equitably, but geared to their strengths.

---

58 Ephesians, Chapter 4:26, 31-32
59 Judith Wallerstein and Sandra Blakeslee, *The Good Marriage*, p. 239.
60 Judith Wallerstein and Sandra Blakeslee, Ibid., p. 239.
61 See: Laura Doyle, *The Surrendered Wife*.

> She realized that the relationship with her husband would be enhanced if she functioned on her husband's strengths rather than his weaknesses. She opted for equilibrium through compromise.

Negotiation

Before accommodation takes place some effort should be expended to discover which of the ten areas of nature and nurture both of you find incompatible. What undesirable behaviors you have developed from them that cause discomfort to your spouse? Once these are determined you can begin focusing on them and negotiating with your spouse.

You may have heard of a win/win situation. That's what is needed in these discussions. Most people are selfish. We tend to think about what affects us. Often in conflicts, the objective is to win the argument. "I am right and you are wrong" is a common attitude in marriage after the early blush of romance is over. Now you must re-orient your thinking to consider that which is good for your spouse, your marriage, and yourself. Your negotiations should reflect that attitude. The aim of negotiation is to settle a disagreement or a conflicting need by finding out what can satisfy both partners. A win/win—i.e., both are satisfied with the arrangement is the outcome that will bring lasting satisfaction. The accommodation reached in such cases will be desirable.

> Now you must reorient your thinking to consider that which is good for your spouse, your marriage, and yourself. Your negotiations should reflect that attitude.

Here are two illustrations: You want to sell your house for $100,000. An inter- ested buyer is willing to pay $90,000. Both may walk away since the prices are $10, 000 apart. However, if both are willing to talk about it and discover what each is willing to accept, a desirable outcome is possible. You may agree at a sale price of $96,000, plus leaving the appliances. If both parties are satisfied with the negotiated agreement, it's a win/win accommodation.

The husband wants to watch a ball game. The wife wants to go to the store to pick up an item advertised for a one-day sale. Both events partially overlap. Instead of fussing about your spouse's lack of cooperation to go with you to the store or your wife disrupting your game, just take a moment and talk about it. See if both can be achieved. If not, go for the next best option. That could be agreeing to miss a part of the game and spending a shorter time shopping.

In a marriage there are several situations that arise that require negotiation. However, if one partner is not willing to negotiate, disappointment and anger may develop in the injured spouse. When that happens frequently, that spouse may withdraw in spirit and later in body as well. Every marriage requires flexibility a willingness to negotiate.

One important rule in a successful negotiation is considering the other party's interest. Most people focus on their own interest only. In that case you do not know what the other party is willing to accept. Let's look again at the real estate illustration. Let's say that the maximum amount available to the buyer is only $96,000. Dropping the price to $97,000 would lose the sale. You need to know what the other party is willing or able to accept. The goal should be satisfaction for both parties, certainly not a win/lose agreement.

The advantage of using the needs assessment to evaluate your desires and those of your spouse is to create a knowledge base in order for you to know your spouse's limitations and strengths. As you negotiate with your spouse you will be more likely to come to a win/win conclusion or compromise.

Let's say the wife believes it is wrong to have sex on the Sabbath (religious day of worship but the husband thinks it is all right. It would be difficult to negotiate on the basis of having sex on Sabbath once per month. Your spouse does not believe it is right. You know that your spouse is a ten on freedom and you are a five. Since you are flexible on freedom but your spouse wants complete freedom to decide his/her actions, you are wise to pull back and negotiate on a different basis. You are more likely to reach an agreement, for instance, with getting her to agree to have sex just before or just after the Sabbath.

> Negotiate wisely before reaching an accommodation. Accommodation should be a win/win situation, not win/lose, or lose/lose.

Being angry with your spouse or pressuring your spouse to do what you desire may prove to be counterproductive or even destructive to your marriage. Yet so many people seek a one-way compromise. Even if the other person gives in to pressure, he/she may be unhappy. Resentment may begin to build up slowly or rapidly build toward an unhappy outcome. Both have lost. Negotiate wisely before reaching an accommodation. Accommodation should be a win/win situation, not win/lose, or lose/lose.

Power Play

Laura Doyle made a great point by using the illustration of the famous dancers Ginger Rogers and Fred Astaire to show the importance of cooperation in order to achieve greatness. She quoted Ginger Rogers as saying, "I did everything he did, and I did it backward, and in high heels." The point is that they both achieved greatness because one allowed the other to lead. Both were great dancers but they had to complement each other, not compete with each other.

> The one who has the least commitment to the marriage has the most power.

When a relationship is locked in a win/lose struggle, it is all about power. One may be asserting it and the other resisting it, or worse, both may be struggling for the ascendancy. The one who has the least commitment to the marriage has the most power. Would you agree?

That explains the reason some marriages end with such bitter feelings. If one party has given up hope and the other is desperately trying to save the marriage, guess who has the least power in the negotiation process? The one who is desperate, of course! The other doesn't care about the outcome since he/she has less invested in its success. If you are more committed than your spouse to the success of the marriage, then you will be prepared to surrender more to reach a solution. The same is true if you want to buy a house and the seller knows you are not prepared to walk away. The seller has you cornered and will not have an incentive to lower the price. That's a win/lose.

Let me use another illustration. My father loved my mother with great passion. When she passed away and left my father with three small children, he felt it necessary to marry again as soon as possible. His new wife had a son my age, a secure job, and her own house. At first, she refused to leave her home to live with us. However, she relented for a short while and came to live in our house. My father could not get a job in the small district where we lived so he accepted a job in a town thirty miles away. His wife refused to move with him. She was more committed to her lifestyle and her son than to the marriage. Needless to say, it was a long struggle before they separated and my father transferred his affection to someone who responded to his needs.

My brother, sister, and I grew up under very difficult circumstances. In my father's second marriage, both partners, perhaps without thinking about it, invested more in their own success and the well-being of their own children than in their marriage. My father was totally committed to our well-being. This is the reason he chose to seek employment elsewhere in order to provide for us. My stepmother, perhaps out of pride or a sense of independence, preferred to keep her job and live in her home rather move with my father. With those attitudes, the marriage was destined to fail. It was a lose/lose situation.

> A successful marriage has at its heart teamwork. Somehow these couples find a way to work things out together.

A successful marriage has at its heart teamwork. Somehow these couples find a way to work things out together. They put emphasis on what's best for the marriage. A marriage cannot last long on selfishness and personal interest.

> Constantly, daily expressing commendation for even little acts or complimenting your spouse for even small deeds goes a far way to provide oil for the machinery of marriage.

Diplomacy

In a Royal Bank of Canada monthly newsletter, the author wrote about diplomacy in marriage. The article stated:

> We pay attention to informing and training of our minds, but diplomacy requires us to educate our hearts. It means not only keeping the home fire burning but throwing a pinch of incense on it once in a while. It includes some kind deeds done for their own sake without expecting a return.
> Even if the bond of family kinship is not so strong as it once was, there is need for the ties of friendship if people are to live happily together, and one of the strong links in friendship is diplomacy. The person who applies diplomacy successfully will not only strew benefits but will reap flowers.

The wise man, Solomon, said, "A word fitly spoken is like apples of gold in a setting of silver."[62]
Constantly, daily expressing commendation for even little acts or complimenting your spouse for even small deeds goes a far way to provide oil for the machinery of marriage.

Biblical Counsel

Even non-religious persons may find that the following two biblical counsels provide wise solutions to marital disagreements. But they must be understood and practiced.

---

62 Proverbs, Chapter 25:11.

1. Paul said:

> …complete my joy by being of the same mind, having the same love,
> being in full accord and of one mind. Do nothing from selfishness and
> conceit, but in humility count others better than yourselves. Let each
> of you look not only to his own interests, but also to the interests of others.[63]

This counsel defies the human spirit. Some people who practice it may do so for the wrong reasons. They may be doing an unselfish thing with a selfish motive.

The *book Bradshaw on: The Family*, which was a New York Times bestseller, was based on a nationally televised series. John Bradshaw argues that the kind of love the Bible advocates and Christians adhere to, which calls for surrendering to each other's interest out of love, is nothing more than codependency. This co-dependency, he claims, leads to dysfunctional families since the parents wreck the family by passing on this "poisonous pedagogy" to their children. He doesn't believe in the "better half" concept and suggests that incomplete people create a dysfunctional relationship in which each convinces the other that they cannot live without each other. He calls this love addiction, similar to alcohol or drug addiction. He claims that those who fall for this logic are destined to marital failure.

I disagree strongly. Whereas the partners should not surrender their principles or give up their rights without principled negotiation, they should be prepared to recognize their partner's weaknesses and give support where needed. The Christian view of marriage is based correctly on the love Christ has for his church. He sacrificed his life for it. When we love each other that deeply, we will not hesitate to surrender our petty selfish desires in favor of our spouse's needs.

2. Paul challenged the Christians with a very important principle. Since Christians should be more sensitive to moral rather than legal remedies for their problems, this challenge should help them avoid divorce. Paul stated:

> To have lawsuits at all with one another is defeat for you. Why not
> rather suffer the wrong? Why not rather be defrauded? [64]

---

63 Philippians, Chapter 2:1-4.
64 I Corinthians, Chapter 6:7.

This means that if each partner in a spousal relationship is prone to forgive and at times even take the wrong, the whole atmosphere in the home will change. If the wronged spouse is ready to forgive, this attitude should help the husband/wife to calm down and respond positively. Even if a positive response does not occur readily, this attitude would be positive for the individual and, eventually, for the marriage.

> If the wronged spouse is ready to forgive, this attitude should help the husband/wife to calm down and respond positively.

Laura Doyle, whose marriage leaped from the pit to paradise, says a surrendered wife is:

> Vulnerable where she used to be a nag;
> Trusting where she used to be controlling;
> Respectful where she used to be demeaning;
> Grateful where she used to be dissatisfied;
> Has faith where she once had doubt.[65]

---

65 Laura Doyle, *The Surrendered Wife*, p. 20.

Chapter Six

Communication

Preview

Some marriage professionals consider lack of communication as one of the leading causes for marital difficulties and marital failure. They believe that communication between spouses leads to healthy marriages. Nevertheless, communication has its shortcomings. Admittedly, communication is important, but frequently it contributes to marital difficulties rather than marital success.

During their communication, people may use the wrong words, give the wrong signals, engage in the wrong attitude, express themselves in the wrong tone of voice, or attempt to discuss vital issues at the wrong time or place. Communication may take place but carry with it unintended results.

Perhaps, you have heard the saying "sticks and stones will break your bones but words can never hurt you." Whoever introduced it has perpetrated a cruel hoax on generations of unsuspecting people. Let's think about a few words we use all the time: no, yes, success, failure, disappointed, and come. Just imagine someone you love or respect using any of those words to you with some emotion. You may either feel elated or dejected. The actions you perform after being told just one of those words could have lasting consequences for you or others.

Let's say you are a promising player on a baseball team at school, in the major leagues, whatever! This is the final game of the season. Winner takes all. You are up to bat. The final out! All your team needs is one run to stay alive or two to win. The bases are loaded. A single will tie and a double will win the game. You are nervous. You attempt to hit three wide pitches and strike out. Do you believe words would matter then?

Let's say that the coach came up to you and said:

> You failed. I will never use you in that situation again. Next time I will
> use someone I can depend on to save the game. I am really disappointed.

He walks away angry and dejected. Consider the other scenario. After you strike out, the coach walks up to you, places his arms around you, and says:

> Come, let's go out for dinner. I still think you are one of the best players on the team. Later, we will take a look at how we can improve. Your success during the season got us to the finals.

Just think for a moment the strongly different emotions you would have simply by the use of a few words. Similarly, if a gentleman who admires a lady for some time and generates enough courage to invite her for a date, there is a big difference between a response of a charming "yes" and a curt "no." Words do mat- ter and how we communicate them matters even more.

> One thing is certain, to be effective, communication between spouses must take into account the other person's needs and views.

Toward a Definition

Communication takes place when a message or information is sent and received. The process is complete only if the information is understood. Albert Ellis and Ted Crawford explain that communication is "mainly to influence others to give you more of what you want, and less of what you don't want."[66]

One thing is certain, to be effective, communication between spouses must take into account the other person's needs and views.

Personal Story

Most of my problems during my marriage were self-inflicted due to ineffective communication. Recently, as I observed our interpersonal reactions within the family more closely, I discovered that all the women in my family circle tend to react to me in a similar manner. They have me doing damage control more often than I care to remember. I usually thought of myself as confident, committed, concerned, correct, and confrontational:

- Confident because I try to get the necessary information before arriving at a decision;

---

66 Albert Ellis and Ted Crawford, *Making Intimate Connections*, p. 28.

- Committed because I am dedicated to giving support and priority to all members of my family at all times;
- Concerned because I always consider their best interest;
- Correct because I usually think I am doing the right thing for them, and
- Confrontational in the sense that I am up-front with my views and I usually challenge theirs without being abrasive.

At least that's how I saw myself. But my family saw my attitude differently. They saw me as aggressive, authoritative, persistent, judgmental, and inflexible. I think my family considered my attitude toward them somewhat like a benevolent dictator. Perhaps, my military training had something to do with it. However, in my opinion, my love and concern for them overshadowed any negative attitudes.

Only recently, I have come to notice the differences in their perspective and mine and I have been making a deliberate effort to adjust. I am more conscious of the way they will react or interpret my remarks. At this stage, my attitude is more preventive than reactive. Maybe the saying that "you can't teach old dogs new tricks" should apply only to dogs. Given the right education and motivation, people can change at any age.

Let me underscore that with an illustration. You will read in many relationship books that you should not expect to change your mate. That's a major point in one of my paradigms and a fundamental principle of Dr. William Glasser's marriage therapy. However, that does not mean that we should not help our spouse to grow and mature in weak areas of his/her life. Just be aware that he/she needs to make the changes. It is not your responsibility to do it for your spouse.

For nearly forty years I encouraged Pam to go on an exercise program, without success. She made every excuse. As one of my New Year's resolutions, I decided not to mention it to her again. Before backing off, I tried one last time to encourage her to go to the gym. To my surprise, she agreed. However, she did not make a specific commitment. In fact, a few years ago she told me about an exercise machine she liked and promised to use it if she had it. You guessed it. I bought it. However, I had to use it myself.

About the time of our anniversary, I drove Pam to the YMCA and parked. She came out with me without comment and interviewed with the agent. We went next to the Gold's Gym. After the interview, we signed up for the program and Pam volunteered to pay the deposit and monthly fees. She went regularly for several months without any prodding from me. She appeared to enjoy the workout. That happened after nearly forty years of prodding! Later, we moved to Jacksonville from Nashville. Without any protest, Pam accompanied me to the YMCA to sign up.

Communication has been one of the key components between Petula and me. Our communication is open and ongoing. Whenever we meet at the end of the day or when I call each night and morning while I am away from home, we share our experiences. We are constantly in touch with each other.

My besetment over the years was my tendency to respond to everything Petula said. My mood would be on display as well. Even if I tried to keep silent, I would break my silence at the wrong time with the wrong words. Obviously, this led to escalation of the foment. Now I try to be more judicious. I listen more and avoid being defensive.

I have found that our disagreements are fewer and less rigid. We are less inclined to be judgmental and critical. Thankfully, the unpleasant times are decreasing and the pleasurable ones are increasing. Here is one communication that worked. It is taken from my book, *Making Marriage Meaningful.*

Recently, my wife [Pam] demonstrated vividly a practical lesson in communication. Something had occurred between us that caused us to lower our usual level of communication, that is, the disruption of our spontaneous spoken and unspoken sharing of our true feelings and thoughts with each other. This lasted about three days. Because we were still relating to each other in a polite way, neither of us attempted to break this mood. One morning Pam took me by surprise. Standing about six feet from me, she held out both her hands toward me and in a gentle voice said: "Take two steps toward me."

I hesitated and beckoned to her to come toward me. She stood firmly in her place and repeated the invitation for me to come toward her. Knowing how determined she is in such situations and feeling a strong impulse to respond favorably to my wife, I smiled and took the two small steps toward her. Then, she took her two steps toward me. We found ourselves in a fond embrace, as we kissed each other as though we were newlyweds.[67]

Problem

I believe the most common cause for a breakdown of communication in mar- riage is moodiness. Of course, there are many other causes: personality traits; frustration caused by problems at work, home, or school; financial difficulties; car problems; illness; and even the weather. There are so many reasons one spouse

---

67 Robert Samms, *Making Marriage Meaningful*, p. 97.

may withdraw into silence. But to me the prominent cause that seems to recur is moodiness or emotional swings.

For men and women there are distinct differences. Because of their different sexual orientation, men and women experience life differently, not only in their sexual experiences, but also in their everyday existence. Differences in the partners' emotional cycles often lay the basis for unexpected misunderstanding and even conflict. The biological (sexual) and emotional curves run along similar lines from woman to woman. The same goes for men. But these fluctuations are radically different for men and women. Psychiatrist Paul Plattner explains the differences of these emotional changes for both men and women. We should try to understand how these differences seriously affect many marriages, sometimes imperceptibly.

Emotional cycle differences often lay the basis for unexpected misunderstanding and even conflict. The biological (sexual) and emotional curves run along similar lines from woman to woman. The same goes for men.

Emotional Curves

Men's emotional peaks and valleys are more frequent, with higher highs and lower lows than those of women. They compare closely to sexual tension and release.

> Man's sexual tension rises from a neutral point zero suddenly and to a very high level. It rapidly achieves its highest intensity and demands release. When release is obtained, a man quickly descends once again to a sexual-erotic zero point....Between these peaks, man is as it were, "empty of love"....In this phase, therefore, he is able to concentrate on factual or spiritual matters, to take interest in things from which sexual love is wholly excluded.[68]

During this "emptying of love" period, a man may pay little attention to his wife and she may consider his treatment to be unkind.

---

68 Paul Plattner, *For Men Only*, p. 63.

The love graph of a woman follows an entirely different design. Once her love is awakened, it remains ever wakeful. She never sinks all the way to that zero point. For a woman love is here to stay. It rises more gradually toward its peak, and, upon release, its descent is also more gradual. Therefore there is nothing purely objective, purely scientific, purely businesslike for her... Therefore she cannot really understand why her husband does not respond to this love, why he hardly even notices her.[69]

Herein lies the problem. When the man is strongly awakened to sexual desire or even affection, his wife may be just beginning to rise emotionally. Because his response is rapid (rapid rise and fall), he may be at the bottom of the desire or response curve when his wife reaches her peak of desire or interest. If they are unaware of these basic built-in emotional and biological curves, then they may be oblivious to the reason the spouse feels or acts in the way he/she does from time to time. The blame game may then present an unnecessary burden on the spouse, who may not even figure out that something is happening in his/her system to cause a mood change.

> When the man is strongly awakened to sexual desire or even affection, his wife may be just beginning to rise emotionally. Because his response is rapid (rapid rise and fall), he may be at the bottom of the desire or response curve when his wife reaches her peak of desire or interest.

This principle should apply broadly to the day-to-day experiences. You never know when these moods will show up. Think for instance about a woman's biological monthly cycle, which also affects her emotionally. What about a man's much shorter cycle of sexual desire? Men and women are much different in this regard. Nature provides that a woman's desire builds up toward a peak monthly in order to provide for pregnancy. After this brief period when pregnancy can occur (a few days), a slow emotional decline and later a slow rising occurs. The same principle applies to sexual activity between the two spouses. The husband and wife are usually on different emotional tracts. The man usually ejaculates much sooner than the woman reaches her climax. He has to make a special effort to wait for her or else she may be left hanging on the edge of a cliff emotionally.

---

69 Paul Plattner, Ibid., p. 64.

Partners must take care to communicate their feelings during this delicate private period.

> He has to make a special effort to wait for her or else she may be left hanging on the edge of a cliff emotionally.

The very important point to observe here is that a great deal of communication and understanding must take place in order that long-term relationship and bonding can emerge successfully. Many marriages break down over this issue and, perhaps, neither partner ever figures out the real reason.

Despite our open society today, we still hesitate to communicate openly about sex between husband and wife, and parents and children. To some extent, we voluntarily remain in ignorance and act as though ignorance is a virtue to be protected with our lives.

> A great deal of communication and understanding must take place in order that long-term relationship and bonding can emerge successfully. Many marriages break down over this issue and, perhaps, neither partner ever figures out the real reason.

Because of our conservative religious background, during much of our marriage, my wife and I rarely discussed certain aspects of sex openly together. We just seemed to avoid it. Bear in mind that everybody's mood is constantly changing. If we are not constantly communicating our feelings, how can we protect and please each other? Usually, if I did what she didn't want at a particular time, she would tell me that I should know what she wants. Maybe so! But I was usually clueless. And I usually responded by asking: "Why don't you just say what you prefer or what you don't want?" Be assured that next time the same thing happened again. Fortunately, we have grown in this area. Our experience is certainly teaching us some wisdom.

In case you have never had that problem and you think we are alone, let me show you that we have company. A woman having a keen insight into this unexpressed communication wrote a book on the issue titled: Men Read Newspapers, Not Minds. Sandra P. Aldrich explains that while teaching high school, she gave only partial credit for incomplete answers. When the stu-dents complained that she knew what they meant, she replied, "No, I read papers; I don't read minds."

She explained further that some wives argue in their heads about how their husbands don't do some things they desired them to do. Using a couple to illustrate her point, she recounts the exchange.

One day, she argued so much in her mind that she finally said aloud to Mark, "It really irritates me that you don't want to go to the antique mall with me!"

He looked around, as though wondering where in the world that comment came from. Then he calmly said, "I didn't know you'd like me to go. You never said anything, so I assumed you liked having that time to yourself."

Now it was her turn to be surprised. "Well, you should have known I'd like you along!"

"Now, Marcie, how could I have known that?" he asked.

"As much as I love you, I can't read your mind."

Marcie gave an exasperated huff. "All right. Would you like to go to the mall with me?"

Mark grinned. "I'd love to, honey. Thanks for letting me know."[70]

Couples who are at a marital impasse discover that their assumptions about their marriage proved to be invalid.

False Expectations

Couples who are at a marital impasse discover that their assumptions about their marriage proved to be invalid. Eric Cohen and Gregory Sterling estimate that the genuine satisfaction between partners ranges between 2 and 10 percent. By comparing the marriage contract to a purchase agreement, they conclude that it is not so much that the fine print is left out of the agreement, but the agree- ment is left out of the communication. They wrote:

Whenever rational reality falls short of expectations, hopes are dashed, resentments flourish, blame is cast and the ensuing conflicts prove to be more than partners can bear—disillusion is almost always the precursor of dissolution.[71]

---

70   Sandra P. Aldrich, Men Read Newspapers, Not Minds, pp. 55, 56.
71 Eric Cohen and Gregory Sterling, *You Owe Me*, pp. 3, 6.

Paradigm Six:

Problem to Solution

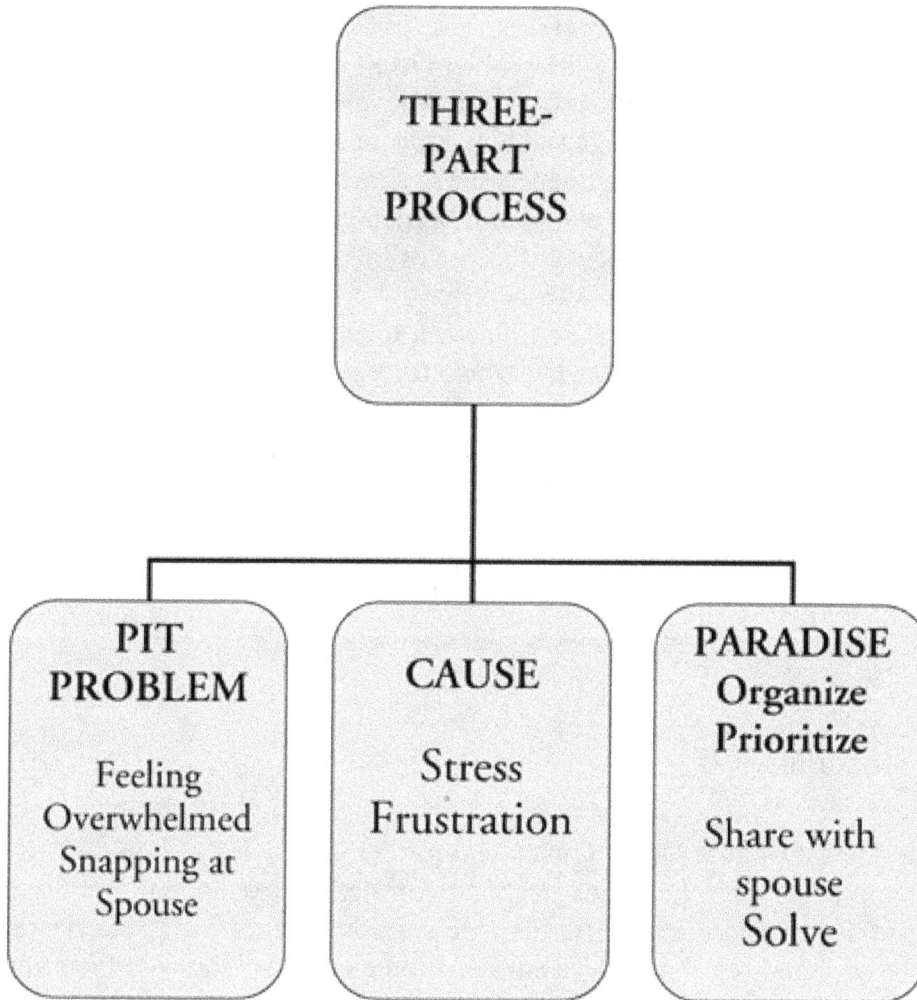

```
          ┌─────────────────┐
          │   THREE-         │
          │   PART           │
          │   PROCESS        │
          └────────┬────────┘
                   │
      ┌────────────┼────────────┐
      │            │            │
┌───────────┐ ┌─────────┐ ┌────────────┐
│   PIT     │ │ CAUSE   │ │ PARADISE   │
│ PROBLEM   │ │         │ │ Organize   │
│           │ │ Stress  │ │ Prioritize │
│ Feeling   │ │Frustra- │ │            │
│Overwhelmed│ │  tion   │ │ Share with │
│Snapping at│ │         │ │  spouse    │
│  Spouse   │ │         │ │  Solve     │
└───────────┘ └─────────┘ └────────────┘
```

Paradigm Six Explained

This paradigm has two three-part processes. The first is the task of discovering the cause or source of the problem, then analyzing the problem itself, and developing a solution. The other process is also solution oriented. When frustration develops as a result of pressure, you organize, prioritize, and share your feelings and plans for solution with your spouse.

Most people get frustrated and experience stress sometimes. In marriage this also occurs. The problem arises, however, when one spouse targets the other spouse in order to vent his/her frustration. Whether the other spouse is guilty or innocent it is likely that he/she will react negatively. This may lead to a fully blown conflict.

This paradigm is designed to provide an outlet, a release valve for couples as they contend with their feelings. First, you consider the cause for your feeling of frustration. Second, you analyze the problem which results or may result. Third, you develop a solution. Rather than snapping at your spouse when you have a demanding schedule which deprives you of quality time to eat or rest, consider:

- Organizing,
- Prioritizing, and
- Sharing your concerns with your spouse.

Providing Solutions

I appreciate the way Laura Doyle guides us into the intricacies of how best wives can get what they want from their husbands without conflict or resentment. In her system, the husband considers it a pleasure to fulfill his wife's needs. The following speaks to the essence of marital relationship. Men should seek similar strategies in dealing with their wives.

Don't hesitate to tell your husband what you want, whether it's a vacation, new furniture, piano lessons for the kids, time to yourself, or even a baby. But make sure you are describing an end result, not telling him how to do it. When you tell your husband what you want without telling him when, why, and how you want him to get it without controlling him, you are giving him a new opportunity to feel accomplished and proud about how happy he makes you. Letting him please you will make you feel adored and intimate.[72]

---

72 Laura Doyle, *The Surrendered Wife*, p. 78.

Several writers have pointed to the problems that develop between spouses naturally because of their gender differences. Knowledge alone, however, is not enough. In fact, most of us know about gender differences instinctively. What is needed is for us to internalize this information, allowing this knowledge to change our attitudes.

Nancy Van Pelt mentioned that ten of her twelve hour-long seminars deal with aspects of understanding the male temperament. When she asks women who attend her seminars the reason they came, "the overwhelming answer has typically been their desire to understand men better."[73] Dr. John Gray said the same about men. Men desire to understand women more. We should make a conscious effort to use our knowledge about the opposite sex to change our attitudes to the opposite sex.

Dealing with the Differences

In his book Men Are from Mars, Women Are from Venus, Dr. John Gray pointed out that men and women are so different in communicating that it is as though they are from different planets and speak different languages. Men and women use language to solve their problems but they use language differently. Dr. John Gray says:

> [Women] use talking as a way of discovering what they want to say;
> and sometimes they talk about their feelings in order to sort things
> out, as a means toward eventually feeling better. At other times,
> women feel a need to share and express their feelings, simply as
> a means to get closer, to experience greater intimacy.[74]

Research results reported in The Shere Hite Report on the Family stresses the view that women want more verbal sharing. They want their partners to express their feelings more often.[75]

---

73 Nancy Van Pelt, *To Have and To Hold*, p. 109.
74 John Gray, *Men Are from Mars, Women Are from Venus*, p. 52
75 Shere Hite, *The Shere Hite Report*, p. 411

> The problem for the unsuspecting husband is that as he tries to solve her problem without being asked to do so he is risking being considered insensitive.

Men's Mistake

Men have difficulty understanding that frequently women talk for reasons other than seeking advice or solution. John Gray puts it this way:

> A man mistakenly assumes that when a woman talks about her feelings and problems his role as listener is to efficiently assist her in feeling better by offering her solutions. Lucky is the man who discovers that satisfying a woman's need to communicate and be heard is the most important requirement in making relationships loving and harmonious. When a man is a good listener, a woman can repeatedly find the place in her heart that is capable of loving him and embracing him just the way he is.[76]

The problem for the unsuspecting husband is that as he tries to solve her problem without being asked to do so he is risking being considered insensitive. The idea is that she would conclude that he really didn't listen. Her real need was to be understood. It is really difficult for a man to listen patiently without listening passively. But he must learn to do so. I have struggled with that for most of my marriage. Although I bear it in mind, even now, I slip up occasionally.

As soon as Pam starts to tell me about a problem at school or an issue with a relative, my mind begins to think of a solution and I have trouble holding back from sharing my opinion. Invariably, as soon as I interrupt her to comment, she gets impatient with me, pointing out that I am not listening. Then the discussion shifts to whether I listened or not. Sometimes she no longer wants to share her feelings on the issue. Knowing where I went wrong, I seek the opportunity to redeem myself and let Pam express her feelings without interruption. The same goes for my daughters. I really have difficulty resisting offering a solution as soon as I hear the problem. Although they don't mind my advice, they much prefer if I listen and give them credit for their efforts toward solving the issue.

Dr. Barbara DeAngelis offers a few secrets about the way women communicate:

---

76 John Gray, Men Are from Mars, *Women Are from Venus*, p. 53

1. Women love to talk because it creates connection.
2. Women express their thinking and feeling process out loud.
3. Women communicate details.
4. Women use talking as a way to release tension.
5. Women minimize how upset they are. Women prefer to create harmony with the man they love.
6. Women internalize their worries, men externalize theirs.[77]

It is obvious that wisdom and patience are needed to effect meaningful communication between the sexes. Next time you hear someone say that a couple needs to communicate with one another, you should remember how difficult this process could become. Effective communication requires time, patience, understanding, and desire.

> Women consider men strong and somewhat invincible. However, men do have a soft side that needs to be protected.

Women's Task

Whereas men do not take the time to listen sufficiently to women, women find men's behavior problematic. Some women cannot understand the reason their husbands don't focus only on them. Part of the reason may be the lack of support he receives from her. Women consider men strong and somewhat invincible. However, men do have a soft side that needs to be protected.

Nancy Van Pelt tells the story of a salesman who lacked his wife's support. He believed in the product he was selling but she constantly undermined his efforts. Despite her lack of support, he advanced to become an executive in a nationally recognized firm. He left her for another woman who gave him support. His wife was flabbergasted.

The reason is simple. Men need someone with whom they can share their failures and successes. They want to share their problems without the fear their wives will crush their spirits. Psychologist Paul Tournier explains that if a man feels his wife is criticizing him, he may resort to an authoritative stance by using sharp words and shut down the discussion. Men are afraid of advice as much as criticism. Here is the reason.

---

77 Barbara DeAngelis, *What Women Want Men to Know*, p. 243.

> A woman for whom everything seems clear-cut, who confidently tells
> her husband how he must act in order to do the right things, no matter
> what the problem may be such a woman gives her husband the
> impression that she thinks him incompetent.[78]

A woman's task is to give her husband affection and support, especially when he is facing difficult challenges.

> A woman's task is to give her husband affection and support, especially when he is facing difficult challenges.

Men are goal or results oriented. Their communication has a purpose. They want the discussion to lead to a solution. That's the reason they are annoyed with women who frequently express themselves without seeking resolution to a problem. Both husband and wife must understand these differences and bear them in mind constantly as they converse together.

If you find this difficult, try to remember how you felt when you just met your spouse. You always wanted to be with each other and share your thoughts and dreams freely without the fear of being criticized or condemned. You were communicating then. Try it again and practice it. Your marriage will thank you.

Deep Listening

Deep listening or listening from the heart with emotional integrity is the basis of emotional support. Deep listening occurs when one listens to the other without passing judgment, offering advice, or attempting to fix a problem. It is the engaged silence that invites your spouse to express his/her deepest feelings sincerely, regardless of what those feelings are. It is not just listening to the story. It is sharing the feelings he/she is having about the story. You can be vulnerable with the confidence that your partner will not demean, criticize or pass judgment. You ask questions or make comments only to clarify what your partner is saying. That's the way you build trust.

> Deep listening occurs when one listens to the other without passing judgment, offering advice, or attempting to fix a problem.

---

78 Paul Tournier, "Listen to Understand," *The Marriage Affair*, p. 31.

You may have different opinions. That's good for the marriage providing the partners allow each other to hold those opinions. Everyone needs to have core values. Those should not be denied.

> You now feel free to verbalize feelings of frustration, anger, and resentment as well as pleasure and happiness. Insights into each other's personality will lead to greater understanding, depth, and emotional satisfaction.[79]
> Communication about such experiences often makes a deep impression on both parties and enriches the relationship. Mutual sharing of personal ideas and feelings is the ultimate goal in marital communication.[80]

Logic vs. Emotion

Attorney Robert Cohen illustrated well how to use logic rather than emotion to gain an advantage and achieve harmony. His wife once burst into his office as he was focusing on a crucial point for an important opening statement for an upcoming court case. She was annoyed that she had to interrupt her shower to answer the phone. He was also upset because he lost his train of thought.

Just before responding to his upset wife, he thought of a solution. He was preparing for an opening statement before the court based on logic rather than emotion. What if he tried the same strategy with his wife? He did. The result was positive. His wife empathized with his side of the episode.

> It is important to remember that both in marriage and in the legal system, a willingness to settle could prove more valuable than risking defeat by holding on to the opinion that you are right.

Attorney Robert Cohen concluded that in court you have to support your argument with facts or suffer defeat. Marriage is no different. It is important to remember that both in marriage and in the legal system, a willingness to settle could prove more valuable than risking defeat by holding on to the opinion that you are right.

Through this poem men may learn a valuable lesson about communication. Maybe one day I'll find a similar poem about how women should relate to their husbands.

---

79 Robert Samms, *Making Marriage Meaningful*, p. 110.
80 Nancy Van Pelt, *To Have and To Hold*, p. 78.

TELL HER SO

Amid the cares of married life, In spite
of toil and busy strife, If you value your
sweet wife, Tell her so!

There was a time you thought it bliss To
get the favor of a kiss;
A dozen now won't come amiss. Tell her
so!

Don't act as if she's passed her prime,
As though to please her were a crime. If
e'er you loved her, now's the time; Tell
her so!

You are hers and hers alone;
Well you know she's all your own; Don't
wait to carve it on a stone; Tell her so!

Never let her heart grow cold; Richer
beauties will unfold.
She is worth her weight in gold; Tell her
so! (Anonymous)

Chapter Seven

Children

Preview

Recently I picked up a small book entitled You Have What It Takes, written by John Eldridge. It's just a tiny book but it tells a father what he needs to know about raising up a son or a daughter. John Eldridge pointed out that every father is duty bound to answer positively over and over his son's life-changing question: Do I have what it takes?

Similarly, he must answer repeatedly his daughter's passionate question: Am I lovely?

Eldridge insists that the future of a father's children is shaped largely by how he responds to his children's yearning for his approval and reinforcement.

The book is about the father's role. No one needs to question the absence of the mother's influence. The saying is still true that "the hand that rocks the cradle rules the world." That's the unchallenged power of mother's influence. But the unique role for fathers in the life of a son or daughter is difficult to replace. We cannot overemphasize the importance of parents' influence during the formative years of their child's development.

In his many publications and radio programs, Dr. James Dobson has been effective in representing positive family relationships. He counsels that in dealing with your children "let love be your guide. A relationship that is characterized by Genuine love and affection is likely to be a healthy one, even though some parental mistakes and errors are inevitable."[81]

---

81 James Dobson, *Marriage and Family*, p. 82.

Personal Story

Freedom

Pam and I disagreed a bit about the method of raising children. Fortunately, we agreed completely on the fundamental principles, such as religious faith, character, health principles, and so on.

However, we had slight disagreement on the issue of freedom. When the children reached ten years of age, I began the process of freeing them from strict parental control. With each of our four children (two boys and two girls), as soon as they reached that age, I sat with them and explained in some detail about sex. Each of them received a book on the subject of sexuality appropriate for their sex and age. The boys got the book *On Becoming a Man*, and the girls got *On Becoming a Woman*.

I made it clear to them that my parental authority would continue until grad- uation from high school or at age eighteen, whichever came first. They were expected to begin assuming certain responsibilities in preparation for taking charge of their lives fully at that stage. Corporal discipline ended at that age as well. Corporal discipline, though rare, was necessary when reasoning was not effective to correct poor behavior.

Pam felt differently. She thought I gave the children too much freedom. But we found a way to accommodate our views. We usually agreed upon the issues that were vital for the guidance of the children. We also disagreed about whether to have disagreements before the children. I felt and still believe that we should not hide our true feelings from the children provided we were careful not to traumatize them. They needed to feel that we were authentic and not trying to hide matters from them. When we held family councils on Friday evenings and Sunday mornings, we allowed them to share in any and all discussions.

> We were united in the view that freedom is one of life's most precious gifts, which should not be denied to our children.

I encouraged them to challenge us on any issue. Sometimes we had spirited debates. Pam felt they should be more respectful to their parents and should not be permitted to challenge our views. Now that they are adults, all four of them have solid core beliefs which they are passing on to their children. They have followed our lead on matters of morality, religious faith, social responsibility, and values. Distance does not separate us. We still function as a close family. As parents, we must have done something right, including praying for them and their children constantly.

Pam and I had frequent debates about the process but never about the principles which formed the foundation of their development. We were united in the view that freedom is one of life's most precious gifts, which should not be denied to our children. Our unshakable commitment was to give them a spiritual foundation on which to build their lives. We accepted and practiced the Biblical counsel: Train up a child in the way he should go: and when he is old, he will not depart from it.[82]

Problem

Many engaged couples dream of a happy home with a loving spouse and chil- dren. Children should be a blessing to the home. However, as most parents have found, children can bring undue stress upon the unsuspecting parents. When children arrive, they are not visiting. They have come to stay. Some children arrive at an inconvenient time. Their demands and irritation can be unrelenting. Apart from that, they are so sweet!

Many parents are not prepared for the responsibility, especially since the children don't come with a manual. (We should concede that all children are different.) With such a formidable task and no specific instructions, new parents find themselves on their own. Often, new parents have more questions and challenges than answers and strategies.

Three Basic Ingredients

Nancy Van Pelt says this:

> Three feelings a child senses significantly affect his comprehension of self-worth: uniqueness, belonging, and human love. These three feelings combine to give stability and support to the structure of the self- concept. If one of these three aspects is weak, to the same degree the developing self-concept will also be weakened.[83]

Let's illustrate with a shocking national tragedy: the assassination of President William McKinley. Nancy Van Pelt gives a profile of the assassin. His name was Leon F. Leon Czolgosz. His parents had immigrated to Michigan just before his birth. His mother died after giving birth to her eighth child when Leon Czolgosz was twelve. Apparently, she was the only one he cherished. He had no friends, except one brother. Nancy Van Pelt writes:

---

82 Proverbs, Chapter 22:6.
83 Nancy Van Pelt, *Train Up A Child*, pp. 32, 33.

The boy's childhood was impoverished. No one cared about him, and
he retreated to a lonely life of self-loathing and personal misery.[84]

Leon Czolgosz retreated into a quiet world of reading radical magazines and newspapers.

Doctrines of anarchism became his consuming interest. His work was
menial and his life as bleak and rigid as the wire he made. [85]

At twenty-five his personality changed and he became depressed and agitated. At twenty-eight he started wandering and attending anarchist meetings. His self- image received another blow when he tried to join a radical club and was rejected.

September 6, 1901, was a beautiful day. President William McKinley was in Buffalo for an Exposition, after which he spent some time shaking hands. Leon Czolgosz had read about his plans in the paper and attended so he could shake hands with the president. But he took a gun.

As the president attempted to shake his hand, Leon Czolgosz fired twice into his chest. He died eight days later. At his trial, Leon Czolgosz told the court:

I saw a great many there saluting him, bowing down to him, and
honoring him. It was just not right.[86]

Prior to his execution, Leon Czolgosz wrote in his confession:

I don't believe one man should have so much ceremony and another
man should have none.[87]

Leon Czolgosz had missed out on the caring, nurturing, loving, and self- esteem that every child should receive from its parents. The tragedy is that many children in our society lack similar parental support and we are seeing the disastrous results. Remember the several school shootings in the United States a few years ago? They were perpetrated by children.

---

84 Nancy Van Pelt, Ibid., p. 25.
85 Nancy Van Pelt, Ibid., p. 26.
86 Nancy Van Pelt, Ibid., p. 27.
87 Nancy Van Pelt, Ibid., p. 29.

Paradigm Seven:
Decision-Making: Willing to Acting

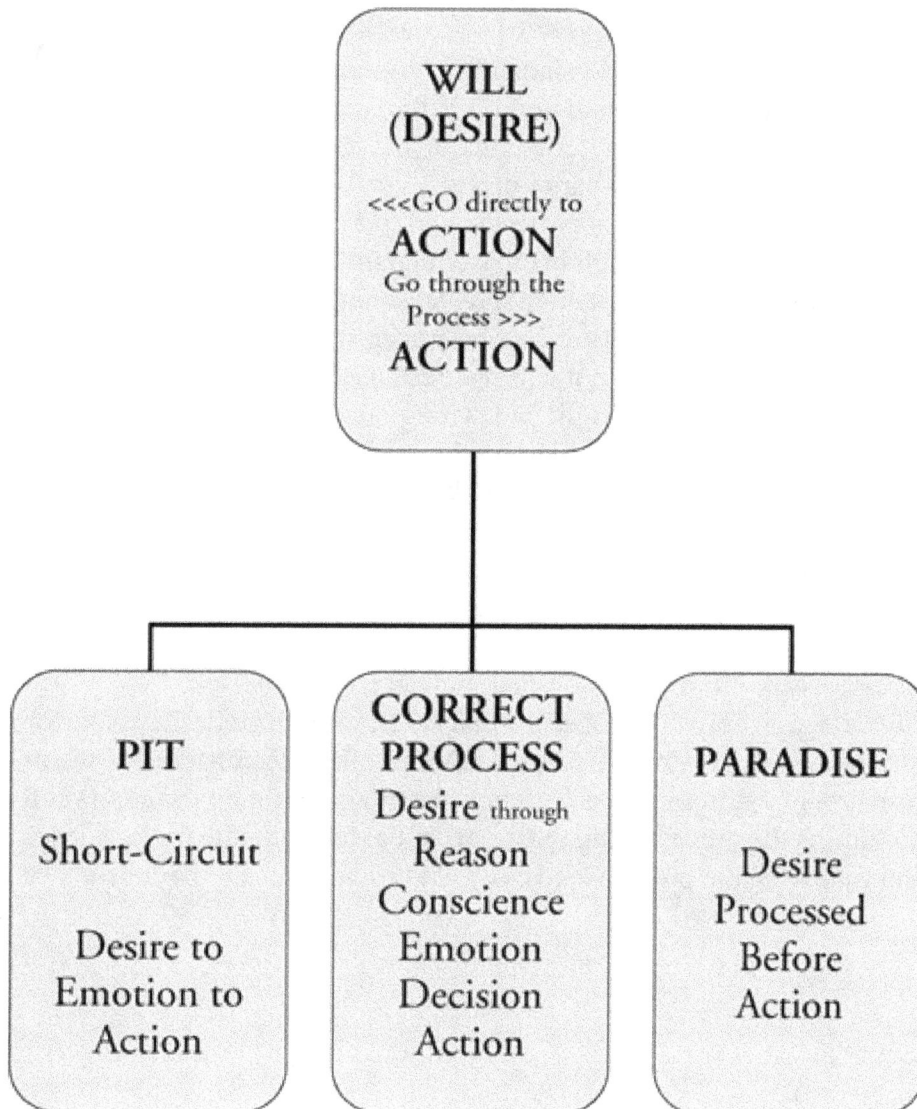

WILL
(DESIRE)

<<<GO directly to
ACTION
Go through the
Process >>>
ACTION

PIT

Short-Circuit

Desire to
Emotion to
Action

**CORRECT
PROCESS**
Desire through
Reason
Conscience
Emotion
Decision
Action

PARADISE

Desire
Processed
Before
Action

Paradigm Seven Explained

About three decades ago, I attended a lecture about the will and the emotions. I don't recall the details but as I reflected on the decision-making process in order to construct a paradigm, I drew inferences from what I remembered.

When you desire to do something (will), you may pass it through your emotion, that is, determine how you feel about it, before going ahead and doing it (action). In that case you give little or no weight to the consequences or morality, i.e., the rightness or wrongness of the action. On the other hand, when you desire to do something, you may choose to process it through your reason (is it wise?) and conscience (is it good?) before acting

Let's say a teenager wants a car in order to pick up his friends, including his girlfriend, to take a joy ride. He can drive but he has no car or driver's license. He could sneak into his neighbor's house and steal his car keys or just hotwire the car and drive away in it. Or, he could choose to pass that emotional impulse through his reasoning and realize that if he meets with an accident the consequences could be devastating. His reasoning could lead him to conclude that the risk is worth the possible pleasure. But then he passes it through his conscience and quickly concludes that the intended action is not worth it because it is not right. After all, lessons taught by his parents gave him a sense of right and wrong and he realizes that he would be risking someone else's property and, perhaps, lives on the road. He decides against the action.

The difference between many of those who make choices that lead them into the pit and those who live wholesome, responsible, successful lives most likely centers on the decision-making process. Many people who create problems in society start from early in life to ignore the process of checks and balances provided by reason and conscience before acting on their desires. They short-circuit the process by going directly from desire to action. Paradigm Seven illustrates how the process of proper decision-making can lead to success.

Looking at the diagram above, we observe that when we will or desire to perform an act, we may choose to go directly to acting upon it (moving left on the chart). Or, we may choose to pass our desire through our reason and conscience (moving right on the chart) before acting. In the center (bottom) is the process available to all of us. Ignoring the process leads to problems and the pit and following the process leads to a wholesome life and paradise.

Providing Solutions

Will (Desire) Controlled by Emotion

When we desire to do something, our will comes into play. As we desire or will to do a particular thing, we may go directly through our emotions to determine if we feel good about doing it. In other words, we allow our emotions to dictate our actions. If we feel like doing it, we do it. The emotions are the seat of our appetite, our joys, sorrows, anger, sex, hunger. Our emotions may be good or bad. In order to act correctly, we need to allow conscience and reason to guide and control our emotions.

The process of avoiding conscience and reason to inform our emotions before acting is followed by people who are immoral or amoral. They can do immeasurable harm to themselves and to their neighbors without much or any internal conflict. In fact, they may try to convince others that they are right in performing their heinous actions. Many of the heroes portrayed in Hollywood movies, as well as real-life murderers, thieves, rapists, prostitutes, pedophiles, despots, totalitarians, etc., use this process with great ease. The prisons are filled with people who have traveled that path successfully until they are stopped. Since the anti- establishment movement of the sixties and seventies, a new attitude has emerged and seems to be prevailing within Europe and North America. It is both overt and covert in its attempts to lead society into an amoral and anti-religious lifestyle. It is a break from absolutes in terms of right and wrong, good and evil to a system guided by a purely humanistic philosophy of what feels good to the individual or the society. The goal is to ignore character building and the traditional approach to processing decisions and to adopt this new philosophy.

The popular utilitarian theory, the subjective theory of relativism, and modern situational ethics form the cornerstones for much of the philosophical basis of modern decision-making. This philosophy is intolerant to religion and moral values. Let me try to simplify these theories and see if you can identify their effects in attempting to manipulate us and our children. See if this thinking does not drive modern education around the world.

Utilitarianism says what is useful is good. It aims to do the greatest good for the greatest number of people. This concept is based on the idea that the ends justify the means. It sounds great until you view it from the perspective of morality and values.

In the modern philosophy, value is considered an object of any interest. This means that the person, persons, or society determine the value. A moral act is defined as the attainment of maximum interest or value. Moral virtue is the realization or development of a habit or state within our nature. Intrinsic value and absolutes concerning right and wrong are eliminated. This modern philosophy teaches that good and evil are relative. You, and the situation you find yourself in, determine the rightness or wrongness of your actions. Since there is no absolute right or wrong, whether you or your children tell the truth depends on the situation in which you find yourselves. According to this modern trend everything concerning morality is relative.

Here are some implications for the family. When applied to sex, situational ethics, the wholesale acceptance of Darwin's theory of evolution, the jettisoning of biblical morality, and the subjective theory of value mean that although man is a complex and developed animal, he is an animal nonetheless. Although few liberal thinkers will admit it, man is expected to act as an animal. Love is simply sexual desire and a romantic feeling is an illusion created by the imagination to increase the value of the loved person as an object of desire. Sex is like any other natural instinct, like hunger or thirst. Although sexual expression can be denied for a time, health requires that it be satisfied as soon as possible after an urge develops. Since it is a need of nature, there is no virtue in restraining it. Just avoid the consequences.

Beginning with the kindergarten, liberal thinkers use every means to convince the educational authorities to desensitize society to moral responsibility, teaching the philosophy that if it feels good, do it. Use sex to pleasure yourself through masturbation, same sex contacts, sex toys, etc. Anyone who disagrees with these views is considered a bigot, ignorant, and not up to date. These modern crusaders label traditionalists as homophobic or religious zealots in order to silence their views. Political correctness seeks to deny freedom of speech to those who resist this emerging trend.

We may recall the controversy which erupted over the remarks of Dr. Joycelyn Elders after a speech at the United Nations-sponsored conference on AIDS in December 1994. Dr. Elders, appointed Surgeon General by President Clinton in September 1993, resigned soon after her controversial remarks. She left the impression that children of school age should be taught about masturbation through what she considers a progressive health agenda. Despite the outcry, she had significant support by the ever-increasing opponents of moral values in the North American society.

> God has made it clear to us that everything we do will have consequences for ourselves and, perhaps, for society. We may disagree with our neighbors' views and lifestyles but we should not restrict their freedom to choose them.

The truth is that those who understand the true biblical teachings should conclude that God has given freedom to every man, woman, and child on this earth to choose how they desire to live. God has taught us by his example that people should be free to lead their own lives and follow their own desires. God has made it clear to us that everything we do will have consequences for ourselves and, perhaps, for society. We may disagree with our neighbors' views and lifestyles but we should not restrict their freedom to choose them.

However, there is a caveat: When their conduct affects others, thereby impinging on the free-dom of others, their conduct becomes questionable. The Bible approves the government's role in regulating society so that everyone can live with a reasonable opportunity to express freedom of choice. A person may choose to believe that pedophilia is a reasonable expression of nature. However, if that person acts upon it by assaulting a child, that person's right to freedom must be revoked and he/she must pay the price for infringing on the child's right to a healthy and normal childhood.

> When their conduct affects others, thereby impinging on the freedom of others, their conduct becomes questionable.

In fact, some ideas are downright harmful to our society. Everyone is entitled to their private views. However, when people teach those views to their children and as a result their children develop rebellious attitudes which may lead to criminal behavior, such as taking a gun to school to harm teachers and other students, society should pass judgment on such teachings or attitudes. Children from homes where their parents teach or demonstrate a lack of moral restraint pass on their poisonous views to others who are susceptible to such influences.

The government should not allow any political pressure to allow unproven theories such as Darwin's theory of the origin of the species, free sex, and subjec tive theories of morality to be taught as fact or settled principle. Similarly, the government should not force children to accept religious values by imposition. Freedom of choice is the right of every citizen. If inconclusive theories or ideas are taught in a curriculum, the other sides of the issue should be given as well. If the theory of evolution is taught, so should the concept of divine origins. The theory of evolution is exactly what its name indicates a theory, not proven science. Why, then, does the school curriculum advance it as settled scientific fact? Similarly, creationism is based on faith. I see no harm in being honest with our children. We should teach both creationism and the theory of evolution for what they purport to be.

The same position should be taken on sex education. If free sex and condoms are introduced, so should abstinence be.

The foregoing philosophies are the driving force behind our modern concept of human behavior. They permeate every aspect of our lives. These modern liberal views have infiltrated our churches. Take music, for instance. Much of religious music is indistinguishable from what used to be considered worldly or secular music. Try to explain the difference to young people. They are growing up in an age when the lines between sacred and secular are blurred or removed. Musical genres now include religious rap, religious rock, religious R&B, New-Age music and a variety of others. There is little or no distinction. This applies to permissive sex and abor-tion. In this permissive atmosphere, how do you teach morality to your children? Let's take a look at the alternative.

The other approach follows the process of decision-making with the checks and balances offered through authentic Christian moral teachings and the constitutions on which our societies in North America were established.

Moral Basis for Decision-Making

In order to act with moral integrity and live by principles worthy of emulation, we must accept, as well as live by, certain common sense, universal truths. Right and wrong, good and evil, truths and falsehoods cannot be denied. We should not allow our emotions to dictate our behavior. We should also educate our reason and conscience so that they will function correctly. Consequently, we will to do good rather than to do evil.

> The other approach is following the process of decision-making with the checks and balances offered through authentic Christian moral teachings and the constitutions on which our societies in North America were established.

Will

The will, or that which we desire to do, must be regulated by checks and bal- ances or informed from some reliable source. All the major religions accept that there is a supreme being, even if they cannot agree on who he is. Most Christians believe there is a God who created the universe, the world, a man, and a woman. He gave the original couple natural and moral laws to govern their existence as well as those of their offspring. After our first parents disobeyed God's rules and committed sin, God decided to send his son, Jesus Christ, to redeem or restore them and their offspring to their original relationship with him. Jesus had to die to accomplish this, because the Bible teaches that without the payment of the penalty for man's disobedience through the shedding of blood, there cannot be divine forgiveness. Christians believe that God revealed his plan for mankind in his communication, called the Bible. The Bible reveals God's will and he invites us, his creatures, to discover his will for us, everyone who is born into the world in order to bring our will into harmony with his will for us.

> Conscience serves to awaken a sense of guilt or render a feeling of peace, satisfaction, and joy as a result of our obedience.

Conscience

The conscience is an inner consciousness that informs our will or desire as to whether our proposed thought or action is right or wrong, noble or ignoble, harmful to others or wholesome. Christianity teaches that the Holy Spirit abides in the conscience to render guidance. Some people refer to this as "the still, small voice." The Spirit guides us along the right path and steers us away from the evil path. The conscience should be educated and carefully protected lest it gives false guidance. The Bible mentions that some people's conscience is like a sensitive skin that is seared by a hot iron. It is healed but leaves a scar that is no longer alive with nerve endings in order to render feeling. That spot on the skin is dead. So it is with the conscience. After enough abuse, it becomes silent or even dies. (See: 1 Timothy 4:2). Conscience serves to awaken a sense of guilt or render a feeling of peace, satisfaction, and joy as a result of our obedience.

Reason

We have a mind or brain in order to analyze and process information. After we inform ourselves with correct knowledge, our wise reasoning educates the conscience, which in turn guides the will. The law of God and the appropriate laws of man, such as the United States Constitution, provide the basis for correct reasoning. The Bible provides the Christian with the source of God's law and examples of wrong and right behaviors and their consequences. So reason must be informed in order to perform its function correctly.

When we receive a stimulus through our emotions or feelings which prompts us to desire a particular thing or to behave in a particular way, we must pass that desire through the conscience and reason before the emotions prompt the final passage of the behavior into action.

We must keep our conscience and reason healthy. We should also hold every emotion in subjection to reason and conscience.

Have you ever wondered why a good person in the eyes of most people, even a president of a country or a minister, commits an evil action? Because of habit! When you allow your will to bypass your conscience and reason and go directly to the emotion, after a while, you develop a bad habit which will allow you to do wrong things without even recognizing it. That's the reason Christians learn to pray daily, asking for divine help to acknowledge and avoid wrong behaviors which may lead to bad habits.

We must keep our conscience and reason healthy. We should also hold every emotion in subjection to reason and conscience. Our actions will thereby become wholesome. That's why we should teach our children good behaviors so that they may develop good habits and sound principles upon which to base their decisions.

Self-Image

I must agree with John Eldridge, who expresses in his book, You Have What It Takes, that fathers have the solemn task of building their children's confidence and self-worth by reinforcing that they have what it takes to succeed in life. Boys need role models to inspire confidence that they have what it takes to become successful men.

Girls need the confidence from home that they are accepted and they are admired. By instilling positive values in their children, parents are equipping them with the confidence they need to face the vicissitudes of life and succeed. A positive self-image leads to developing self-respect.

Parents' Responsibility

Parents should not only help their children develop noble characters, but they should assist them in developing intellectually. Pam and I taught all our children to read. With regard to their education, I was responsible for the two older ones and Pam was in charge of the two younger ones. We were busy but we supervised every aspect of their education, including keeping constantly in touch with their teachers.

Parents should not only help their children develop noble characters but they should assist them develop intellectually.

Personal Story

Let me present a few examples from the experiences of our four children as they went through school in order to demonstrate that we took our role as parents seriously. A key role for any parent is to guide their children through the maze of youthful challenges so that they can experience a soft landing when they approach adulthood. If parents are not present to help when their children stumble, the children will most likely fall. The hurt may prove fatal. Be there consistently for your children and, when appropriate, be there for your grandchildren, too.

1.Richard at Wagar High School

He was entering grade nine. He had completed the grades available in the private church school where he got mostly A's on his annual reports. But soon after he enrolled in the new school, I was informed that he failed the class entrance test for his grade in French, biology, and history. Since his former school had recommended him for an advanced grade level and the test was based on that level, the school administration decided to place him in a grade level commensurate with his performance on the test.

I appealed to the school counselor and teachers to give him a chance to adjust to his new school but they were determined to proceed. Without probing to discover that he was unaccustomed to a large school setting and needed time to adjust, they concluded that he was incapable of coping with the grade level to which he was recommended from his former school. I made an appointment with the principal, who dismissively sided with the teachers. He supported his decision with the test results he was given.

Located in one of Montreal's wealthiest neighborhoods, Wagar High School was reputed to be one of the best schools in the city. The administration was fixated on maintaining this reputation. I was concerned that the disappointment would af-fect Richard's self-confidence. This could affect his performance. With no other avenues available to us, I threw the principal a challenge: "Repeat this test in two weeks and I will accept your decision then." Surprisingly, he accepted.

I took Richard's textbooks and worked with him after school each night and weekend for two weeks. When he was retested, he passed and was pro- moted to the higher grade level. By the way, the history class was studying the Canadian constitution for that term. Richard made an "A" at the end of the term. Later, he attended Vanderbilt law school. Currently, Richard and his wife, Alicia, operate their own law office.

2. Tammy at Harry Ainley High School

Tammy lost interest in math during her senior year in high school. The problem was not the subject but the teacher. I don't recall the details but I remember that she refused to return to her math class. This meant that despite her good grades during high school, she would not graduate with the official government high school diploma.

After exhausting all the usual strategies I could think of to change her mind, I offered her something I knew she wanted. I promised to send her to spend some time with her cousins in Miami after graduation. She accepted.

We went together to see the teacher. I explained her frustration with his course and offered to give her every support at home if he would give her better attention in class. Tammy completed the math class and passed her provincial exam and graduated. I fulfilled my promise to send her to Miami for a few months. Today, Tammy holds two master's degrees from Columbia University and directs a youth remedial program in Brooklyn, New York.

3. Royland at Westminster Elementary School

Pam, who supervised the two younger children's schooling, met with Royland's teacher after he had been given a low grade in one of his classes. Knowing his capability, Pam asked the teacher to show by his assignments and tests how she computed the grade. She was unable to do so. She corrected his grade. He was taught to be respectful so he was reluctant to challenge the teacher. He chose to rely on his mom for assistance because he knew he would get the support he needed to deal with the problem at school.

When Royland completed two years of college, he told us he was tired and wanted to work for a while before continuing in college. Although he was still functioning from home, he was given full autonomy to choose his next direction. However, we counseled him to complete college before taking a break. He agreed. As I expected, he never took the break he thought he needed. Instead, he went on to complete his professional studies. Today, as a doctor of optometry, he and his wife, Shawna-rika, run their own highly successful practice.

4. Sherine at the Crossroad

Sherine was a gifted all-round student. She was an athletic star throughout her high school years. She was also an honor student. She was offered a sports scholarship to attend Purdue University but she declined because the school could not guarantee that she would not have to compete on her Sabbath. The recruiters appealed to us as her parents to convince her to accept but we insisted it was her decision. Although she was excited about the opportunity, Sherine held to her religious conviction and chose to decline the proposed scholarship. She paid her way through college with our assistance. Today, Sherine is dedicated to her career as a vocal musician.

I can't soon forget the drama Pam and I had when Sherine reached her senior year in college. Although she had achieved an excellent grade average, she surprised us when she decided not to return to college for her final year. I was concerned because she showed signs of burnout. Yet I didn't want to give up without trying. I suggested that we take a look at the school bulletin to see which of the programs she could complete with the least stress based on the subjects she had completed. We found that political science would require the least number of compulsory courses and would be a good preparation for law.

During the school year, I gave her close assistance. It was a special treat to attend Sherine's graduation. We were thrilled to see her graduate. Because she was previously a music education major and had distinguished herself as a vocalist, Sherine was selected to sing at her graduation with about twenty thousand attendees crowding the huge stadium.

Parental Support

I trust that relating episodes in the lives of our four children serves to demonstrate the constant need for parental guidance. During the formative years when they were given moral and spiritual training, we taught them to believe in divine intervention in their lives. As parents we were constantly aware that they needed continuous close supervision and guidance in order for them to develop sound characters and the passionate desire to succeed and contribute positively to the lives of their fellow citizens.

Parents are responsible for attending every parent-teacher conference, visiting the school when questions arise, assisting and supervising homework, and seeing that their children attend to all aspects of their school program. They should patiently and tactfully guide their children through school to the completion of college. If they don't have the skills, a family member or friend should be invited to assist.

Parents are responsible for their children's health and social relationships. They should help their children develop healthy habits in eating and caring for their bodies. Effort should be made to dine together as a family at least once each day and hold a family council once per week. During these family connections, parents may pick up meaningful signals to help them zero in on issues in their children's lives. These are times for sharing, planning, and counseling. The place where your children grow up is vital to the influences that will affect their character. Their self-image will be shaped by their surroundings as well. The Greek philosopher, Plato, espoused a vital principle in his *Republic*:

> When youths are surrounded by beautiful objects and noble persons in life, art and literature, they learn to delight in goodness and beauty and [are] repelled by ugliness and baseness. The best education is not that by precept and exhortation but by continuous association with good men.

Parents are responsible for giving their children a spiritual foundation. All of us need an anchor in life. Some people try to go through life without a moral compass but often they are like a small ship caught on the vast ocean in a raging storm.

> Children left to their own devices without moral training and discipline will embarrass their parents, prey upon their neighbors, and wreck their own lives. To have a positive, purpose-driven life should be the goal of everyone on earth.

Ellen G. White, perhaps the most prolific female writer of the two previous centuries, penned this counsel for the youth.

> The natural mind leans toward pleasure and self-gratification. It is Satan's policy to manufacture an abundance of this. He seeks to fill the mind of men with a desire for worldly amusement, that they may have no time to ask themselves the question: how is it with my soul? The love of pleasure is infectious. Given up to this, the mind hurries from one point to another, ever seeking for some amusement. Obedience to the law of God counteracts this inclination, and builds barriers against ungodliness.[88]

Children left to their own devices without moral training and discipline will embarrass their parents, prey upon their neighbors, and wreck their own lives. To have a positive, purpose-driven life should be the goal of everyone on earth. The

----

88 Ellen G. White, *Messages to Young People,* p. 386.

Biblical King Solomon had all the beautiful women he wanted, all the wealth he desired, and all the power anyone would seek. Yet Solomon concluded:

> Let us hear the conclusion of the whole matter: Fear God, and keep his commandments: for this is the whole duty of man. For God shall bring every work into judgment, with every secret thing, whether it be good, or whether it be evil.[89]

---

89 Ecclesiastes, Chapter 12:13, 14.

Chapter Eight

Family Finance

Preview

Apart from infidelity or tragedy, I can consider no greater potential burden to a marriage than financial problems. During the early years of my childhood money was not given the exalted place it has today. Our family and most of our neighbors grew and raised most of their food. They also made most of their clothes. They obtained water from the nearby underground spring, which was clean, clear and refreshing, or collected it in drums when rain fell. Donkeys were truly beasts of burden, used to haul food, water, and other goods and provided an inexpensive means of transportation. The limited need for money was provided by the sale of crops naturally grown or cultivated. Today it is different, much different.

Money had little impact on families in those earlier generations. Today, money has a major role in the functioning of most families. Money may impose itself on the family as a blessing or a burden.

Personal Story

My goal was to live debt free as my parents and grandparents did. That was before I discovered credit cards, or more correctly, credit cards discovered me. Because my credit was excellent, companies sought me out and enticed me with the idea of free money. I had a big family so I obliged the credit card companies at first by getting one or two cards. Everything went great. In fact, I nearly paid off the mortgage for our house in Montreal. Everything continued quite normally for a few years until "Mr. Murphy" paid us a visit.

Ever heard of Murphy's Law? Everything that can go wrong will go wrong! I leave the rest to your imagination. In 1981, our incomes changed. Our family moved from Montreal to Alberta in Canada. My wife (Pam) went back to school to obtain her teacher's certification for that province. The children became teenagers, thereby creating new financial demands. We had moved to Alberta just prior to its economic collapse and we were caught in the aftermath. Like magic, what we considered to be free money now became an albatross around our necks. Not to be defeated, I created ingenious means to survive and emerge from the jaws of financial defeat. After that experience, I vowed not to rely on credit cards. I slipped and fell a few more times by rationalizing that I would use credit wisely. But it never worked. Despite our best efforts, the credit cards would soon start a steady climb toward their credit limit. Many years ago, Pam and I decided we had enough. We abandoned the use of credit purchases.

So if you have more expenses each month than income, don't be too quick to blame your income. Look hard, very hard, at your expenses.

I also had to learn some techniques in dealing with money in our relationship. I found that Pam and I had radically different philosophies of shopping. When I need something, I go to the store, buy it, and get out. Pam stopped at several departments in the store before getting to what she entered the store to buy. Sometimes, she even neglected to follow through to seek the item for which she entered the store in the first place. I still can't get used to that. But Pam always wanted me to accompany her on this meandering journey through the aisles.

Earlier in our marriage, I would be upset when Pam bought items I considered unnecessary. Consequently, I annoyed her with my concern and caused my lovely wife to be upset. Sometimes, we took days to get over our hurt or angry feelings. The main reason was that Pam didn't see any reason to change and I felt she should. Unfortunately, a solution would not be reached soon. It came many years later. Be assured that Pam was a diligent worker and deserved every item she purchased. Nowadays, I tell myself, "It's only money." That's what I say when an unexpected car bill hits, my cell phone bill is twice the monthly charge, or other surprise expenses torpedo my finances. Saying that with any sincerity I can muster causes me to feel better immediately. Don't get upset with your spouse over money. It's not worth the stress.

Fortunately for us, I don't really have to care much what financial choices Petula makes. There are two reasons: we have learnt our lessons about debt and she is as committed as I am to avoiding debt. Furthermore, she is a very careful shopper.

Problem

Our society has imposed a spending culture upon individuals and families. Most people now purchase items impulsively because of massive advertising. Many get in deep debt before they realize what is happening to them. College youth, for example, are burdened with credit card and student loan debts before they even start earning. Most people in debt have a mindset which encourages them to continue on the same path. They curse their fate but refuse to change their mindset.

The purpose of this chapter is to offer a better way to those open to change, radical change.

"When it is dark enough, men see stars." Ralph Waldo Emerson

Paradigm Eight:
The Debt Trap vs. Financial Freedom

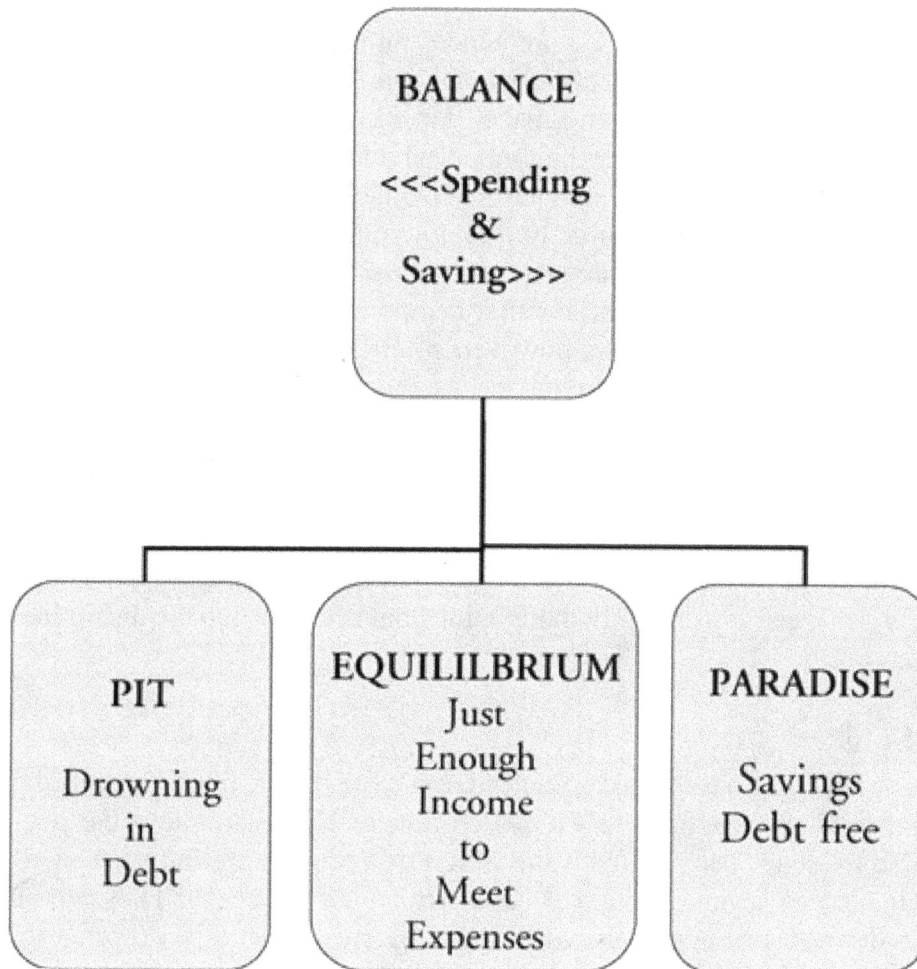

BALANCE

<<<Spending
&
Saving>>>

PIT

Drowning
in
Debt

EQUILILBRIUM
Just
Enough
Income
to
Meet
Expenses

PARADISE

Savings
Debt free

Paradigm Eight Explained

Most people would like to have extra money in the bank or at least more money each month than their expenses. However, many people find themselves with a growing debt that threatens to drown them. Paradigm Eight helps couples to focus on the need to eliminate debt and live debt free. This chapter tackles the way to accomplish that forbidding task.

Uncontrolled spending leads to indebtedness and the pit. Moderate spending may lead to just getting along financially. Saving some of your income, rather than spending it all, leads to financial peace and prosperity.

Earning and spending have enormous influences on a couple's relationship. This influence may be greater than most couples realize. Money's influence crosses boundaries into nearly everything we do and every decision we make. It is a kind of silent partner in the marriage relationship. Therefore, getting and spending money should be taken seriously if the relationship is to be successful. Paradigm Eight illustrates that debts and uncontrolled spending may cast an undue influence on your marriage, directly through your spending, and indirectly through the pressures of debt when funds are inadequate for normal functioning.

When couples become unhappy and conflict begins, the marriage may be heading for problems and the pit. By living debt free, however, couples will be free from financial pressures and have disposable funds to meet everyday needs, thereby eliminating a major irritating cause for marital conflict. Such couples are on their way to peace, pleasure, and paradise.

The center column reflects the status quo. The couple is neither hurting financially nor saving. They are just getting along. If a large financial emergency hits, they will move quickly to the left on the chart. They will be in debt and in danger of the pit. If they get some significant increase in income, they could move toward the right on the chart. They will be in a position to save and enjoy debtfree status. Mainly though, the goal is to develop the discipline to eliminate debt and save.

Providing Solutions

The issues for this topic have been introduced. Let's see if we can find some solutions. I once read about a prison that confined rebellious criminals. The guards told the prisoners that it was impossible to escape because the walls were fortified with reinforced steel. The prisoners accepted their fate for several years and never attempted to escape. They thought the effort useless. One day the guards announced that the prisoners would be escorted to their newly built fortified prison. Before leaving the old prison, the guards showed the prisoners the folly of believing their situation to be hopeless. They made sure the prisoners saw them use their fists to punch holes through the cardboard walls of the cells. The stunned prisoners looked on with consternation. The walls were painted to appear impenetrable. The prisoners were held captive within these weak walls only by their own minds.

What lessons can we learn from this illustration? Most people live their entire lives in one type of voluntary bondage or another. Those who know me will attest to the fact that I have lived my life with the idea that we can accomplish much more than we attempt. Whenever I was assigned a major task, I immediately pulled it apart and then started to rebuild with the express aim of making it better. My entire career, from my first job out of college onward was spent in leadership—creative leadership.

Those who have a desire to succeed must approach life in a similar manner. Nature is in a constant state of change. We cannot resist natural change but some people resist mental change or growth. Most people who set their minds to it can escape poverty and debt, at least in North America, where freedom is cherished.

The poet Robert Browning captured the essence of my motivation over the years and I trust his thought will inspire you to greater accomplishments.
"Ah, but a man's reach should exceed his grasp or what's a heaven for?"

Spending: Getting in and out of Debt

What Is Debt?

For some people, indebtedness is when you can't pay your bills. A friend once told me the story of a frustrated man who had too many creditors. He devised an unwise survival scheme. Putting all his bills in a hat at the end of the month, he drew randomly to see which ones got paid that month. On one occasion, a creditor called and pressured him to pay. He told the creditor, "If you call me one more time, your name will not even get into the hat."

Debt has many forms. Jerrold Mundis, who wrote a book based on the principles and techniques of Debtors Anonymous, defined debt this way:

- Any amount of cash you borrow without putting up collateral,
- Any credit extended to you,
- Any service you take without paying for it at the moment you receive it.[90]

---

90 Jerrold Mundis, *How to Get Out of Debt, Stay Out of Debt, and Live Prosperously*, p. 15.

In a strict sense, secured loans are not debts. You owe the money but the lender holds a collateral or something from you, which has equal or greater value than the amount of the loan. If you default, the lender can claim your asset. With the exception of large purchases such as a house, even secured loans should be avoided because in most cases the lender does not want to claim your asset, unless it is liquid asset (that which can be easily converted into cash, such as a certificate of deposit. Furthermore, you want to honor the arrangement. So the amount owing is an obligation.

Most people get into debt without knowing it. Because you can pay your bills, you don't worry about it. But what happens when your income drops and you can no longer pay? Suddenly, you realize you are in debt. But you were in debt all along. Many people are only one crisis from bankruptcy. When you have to borrow to pay your bills, you are really in debt.

When I served as treasurer for a large church organization, I observed to my dismay that before the end of each month a few of the retired ministers came to my office to pick up their paychecks. I was only twenty-eight years old and couldn't understand the reason professional people spent all their mature years working and yet, after retirement, they had insufficient funds to carry them to the next paycheck. Now that I have reached the age of retirement, I understand the reason for the problem. The fault lies squarely at the feet of poor spending habits.

So you find yourself gradually being squeezed more and more by debt. You have less income than expenses. Your month is longer than your money. Creditors phone you at dinner time, early in the morning, and late at night. You stop answering the phone. You begin to borrow money to pay your bills, get another credit card, or you are just barely able to pay your bills so far. Murphy's Law hasn't visited you yet. When it visits unexpectedly with one emergency, you will be cornered financially. You find that you and your spouse are having more frequent arguments and blame is flowing freely. You are angry at your children for the slightest misstep on their part. Basically, you are miserable. You know you deserve to buy a needed item but you can't, or you do, and sink yourself further into debt. You are finding out that, as one person said, "Money talks but often it is saying, 'Good-bye!'"

You ask yourself, "How did I end up in this financial bind?" You don't need someone to tell you how it happened. Nor do you need sympathy from someone else in the same despair. Nor do you need pity from those who seem to be financially free. What you need is a strategy to get out of debt and begin saving for your future.

"Whatever the mind of man can conceive and believe, it can achieve." Napoleon Hill (Think and Grow Rich

About ten years ago I heard for the first time a radio program based in Nashville, Tennessee, called Financial Peace. The radio host, Dave Ramsay, explained how he had built a real estate empire only to see it collapse during the eighties economic downturn. After fighting his way back to normalcy, he wrote a book called Financial Peace and launched a radio program to alert the public to the destructive nature of debt any form of debt. Dave Ramsay speaks from a Christian perspective and believes in supporting his church and other charitable organizations. But he is dead set against credit cards. Today, Dave Ramsay's program is nationally syndi-cated, his book is a bestseller, and his financial seminars are in great demand. Many others are holding seminars on this topic getting out of debt. Why? Many of the TV evangelists empha-size getting wealth or achieving financial freedom. Why? More and more people are finding themselves in debt and finding it difficult to escape once the crisis begins. Some give up and declare bankruptcy and start the same cycle all over again. Others seek debt coun- seling. Still others give up the struggle and just hide from the creditors.

By the way, bankruptcy to avoid your honest debt should not be an option for an honest person. Of course, there are circumstances which are unavoidable. But this is not the case for most people who declare bankruptcy. I rented property at one time. Tenants would refuse to pay. When I tried to collect the months of overdue rent, they declared bankruptcy to escape payment and live in the property longer. I got out of the real estate business because I didn't have the heart to evict people who were crying and telling me they lost their job or they had nowhere to take their children. My wife forbids me to own rental property. She claims my heart is too soft. She is right.

Since I have a financial background, I had the interest to review several debt- free strategies. I am fully convinced that most people who are prisoner to debt can in a very short while become financially free. No matter how much debt you owe or how bad your credit, in a short time you can begin to pay cash for all your purchases and live debt free. You just need to follow a few steps. Those who will succeed and enjoy a better future must change their attitude radically.

> No matter how much debt you owe or how bad your credit, in a short time you can begin to pay cash for all your purchases and live debt free.

I will not deal with financial investment since it is outside the scope of my present objective. To be candid, investment is not my area of expertise. What I will do is offer some sound suggestions in addressing family financial strategies on how to live debt free.

The indispensable factor in getting out of debt is to decide today to do a paradigm shift: even if your situation is not desperate, if you live on borrowed money, you need to change your concept of spending. First, you must admit you need to change. Then, say out loud to yourself:

Today, I begin paying off my bills. Today, I begin getting out of debt. When

you convince yourself that you are ready to change your way of dealing with your finances, you are ready to get out of debt. Benjamin Disraeli said, "Nurture great thoughts, for you will never go higher than your thoughts."

So you ask yourself pointedly: Where did all the money go? To answer that question, you need to take an inventory. Be brutally honest with yourself. Make a list of everything you spent during the previous month. Spend time to recall every expenditure you made. Now make a list of your living expenses. Don't include the debts, only living costs rent/ mortgage, food, transportation, etc. Leave out car payments, but you can include a reasonable depreciation on your car. Leave out frills, such as dining out or tickets to the concert, any expense that you can live without. Your list should include only the real basic needs to function normally, if you had no debt, even car payment. The idea is to discover how much you are spending above your basic needs at your present living standard if you had no debts. Deduct the latter from the former. The difference is the amount of expenses created because of your spending habits. Even if you had bills from emergencies, the result is the same because if you had the proper spending habit you would be able to cover your emergencies with reserve funds. Of course, I am not referring to a crisis, such as incapacitating physical injury.

Do you realize that two salaries are sometimes less than one? Let me illustrate with a couple's experience detailed by Linda Kelly.[91] The husband earned $30,000 annually. They agreed that the wife would go to work and get a sitter for the children. She got a job for $20,000 annually. With extra money, (about $800 they decided to:

- Get a larger house ($300 more monthly);
- Begin a savings plan for the children ($200);
- Have a comfortable amount of spending money ($300).

When they calculated the cost incurred for the second income, they found that child care, house cleaning services, personal upkeep, transportation, taxes

---

91 Linda Kelly, *Two Incomes and Still Broke*, pp. 15ff.

and Social Security, increased tax bracket, etc., added up to $1,867. The wife's monthly income was $1,667. The difference is minus $200. To the couple's amazement, not only did they not have any money left over, her job created a deficit in their budget of $200. So it cost the family an extra $200 per month for the wife to go to work.

Have you ever calculated the cost to your family for having a second income? You may be surprised.

You may think that I am talking about eating cat food to get out of debt. Not at all! You will have to make some sacrifices but the process could be fun, especially when you see the debts disappearing one by one. Now let's begin.

- *Stop spending* on credit immediately.

If you can manage to start this program without outside financial assistance, do so. If you are too burdened in debt to do so, then consult a debt counseling service. Don't think they can't help. They can do some things that many people can't do for themselves. They can get creditors to reduce your debt or lower your interest rate; hold off your creditors, and restructure your payments to fall within your income. They really can help. Choose the right one carefully by first interviewing them or getting a recommendation.

> If you have credit cards, cut them up immediately.

- Cut up all credit cards

If you have credit cards, cut them up immediately. Or if you are scared, follow an idea I picked up some time ago. Destroy all your cards but hold onto one for emergencies, real emergencies. Place it in a container and fill it with water. (Leave air space in the container for expansion after freezing.) Place it in the freezer. You will think a few times before taking it out to use it. The important thing is you have to be radical with credit. It can be blamed for much of your debt. It allows you to buy on impulse, buying things you can do without, and it punishes you with excessive interest.

> The important thing is you have to be radical with credit. It can be blamed for much of your debt. It allows you to do impulse buying, buying things you can do without, and it punishes you with excessive interest.

Here is my reasoning. When I owned credit cards, no matter how I tried to avoid using them I found a way to convince myself that it was necessary. Eventually, no matter how many cards I had, they ended up near or at the maxi- mum. And they never go down and stay down. So one day I asked myself, why use a means of purchase that charges so much interest (about 20 percent) and is near the maximum anyway? The same money I used to pay interest I could use at my discretion to purchase items without incurring debt obligation.

Now I use only a debit/Visa card, which does the same thing as a credit card and I have no obligation. For auto rental, I use a prepaid Master Card when the debit card is not accepted. I always carry a reserve means of payment anyway, in case something goes wrong with the use of my bankcard. (Murphy's Law is the chief culprit. When I am unprepared, something usually goes wrong.) Using a debit/Visa allows me the discipline to spend money I have in the bank or I am forced to walk away. The feeling of freedom is enormous. It took a long time to convince Pam to do the same. Now she is fully convinced and even though she can pay off her credit card every month she would not go back. Paying off your card every month is a promise that few people who are struggling financially can keep. So if you want to live debt free, the cards must go. The store cards are included. They are the worst for interest.

- List in detail all you spent for the previous month

It is difficult to attack a problem if you don't know what it is. When you see or feel the problem, you know it is real. But you need to bring it out into the open so you can confront it. Your goal is to destroy it. You need to look squarely at the beast. Add up all your current payments and see how much you really spent for a month. Remember to include unbudgeted items, such as the purchase on your way from work, pizzas, snacks, etc. Compare the total amount spent for the month to your income. (This list is different from the list you made earlier.) Do you have more income than expenses? If so, is it sufficient to set some funds aside for emergency or investments?

- Make up an assets and liabilities statement

Take two sheets of paper. On the top of one write "Assets" and on the other write "Liabilities." This exercise is very important. It will show you your true financial status. Under "Assets" list everything you own that you could reasonably sell, if you had to. In other words, would someone be interested to buy it and for how much? Leave out personal items such as clothes. Include house, car, furniture, etc., at the price someone would be willing to pay should you choose to sell them. Don't consider what you feel it's worth. That could be too emotional.

Don't worry whether you owe a balance on the item, such as the loan on a car. Just put the value. Did you remember pension savings? You should be able to look at the list and see everything you own. Add up the list. The total represents your assets.

Now take the sheet marked "Liabilities". List all your debts regardless how small and to whom it is owed, even if it's your mother. If you are obligated to pay it back, list it. You should include your mortgage, auto loan, all credit cards, etc. Add up this list. The total represents your liabilities.

After adding up both lists, determine which is larger. Deduct the smaller from the larger. If the assets total is larger, the difference is your net worth. That's truly what you are worth financially. If the liabilities total is larger, the difference is the extent to which you are indebted. You may be considered bankrupt because your liabilities exceed your assets. If someone were to take all you own today and sell it to pay the bills you owe, would the bills be paid off with cash left over? Or would they have to go to your nearest relative to get the difference? Or, as they did in Bible times, would they sell your family members in slavery or throw you in jail until you pay? (I haven't been able to figure that out. How can you pay if you are in jail?) Anyway, by this you know exactly your financial position. If you are in debt, ask yourself what you must do to change it.

1. Remember, you begin by stopping the spending immediately. You don't stop drinking by having that last drink.
2. Open a savings account and try to build it up to $500–$2,000 depending on your situation. This should be done as soon as possible. Refrain from using this fund unless you have an emergency, a real emergency.
3. Dave Ramsay and other financial advisors recommend that everyone make a budget. But I don't like to decide my daily life by a budget. It's too restrictive for me. Jerrold Mundis understands my pain. In advising how to get out of debt, he suggests a spending plan, not a budget.

He says:

> A budget confines you to a dark little room while everyone else is outside playing in the sunlight. It's no wonder that most people are depressed by budgets and don't stay with them very long.
> A plan on the other hand, is a detailed scheme, a method worked out beforehand to accomplish a goal. A general doesn't budget a victory, he plans a victory. A lover doesn't budget a romantic night, she plans a romantic night. The distinction is important. There's a world of psychological difference between a plan and a budget.[92]

---

92 Jerrold Mundis, *How to Get Out of Debt, Stay Out of Debt, and Live Prosperously*, pp. 128, 129.

The Spending Plan is a set of guidelines you establish to assist you to control your spending. You decide beforehand what you will include in your spending and what you will exclude. No more impulse purchases. You are on a mission. And you must adhere to the guidelines in order to succeed. Your plan should be flexible enough to conform to your changing needs. Eliminate all spending you can avoid. Stick with the basics. Remember this is only for a limited time; you will soon be free financially.

> The Spending Plan is a set of guidelines you establish to assist you control your spending. You decide beforehand what you will include in your spending and what you will exclude. No more impulse purchases.

Rework your spending plan to fit your net income. Leave as much room as possible for savings to begin. You may need to sell some items, get an extra job, even move into a smaller house or own a less expensive car.

4. Paying Off Your Debts

Make a list of all your debts. Arrange them in order from smallest to largest. Now you are ready for the real surgery. You target the smallest one and pay it off as soon as possible. Since you place spending on hold, you can use all available funds to pay on your bills. Pay the minimum payment required on the other bills and concentrate on the smallest. When you pay off the smallest bill, start on the next smallest by putting the money you were paying on the one you just paid off on the one which has become the smallest. Then go to the next smallest, and the next, and so on.

> Pay the minimum payment required on the other bills and concentrate on the smallest.

You will notice a snowball effect taking place. Your sense of satisfaction will begin to build as you continue this process. As you pay off each bill in this way, you will have larger and larger amounts to pay on the next one in line until you are left with the largest bills. Because you are paying larger and larger amounts, even those will disappear shortly.

The advantage of this approach is that you are reducing your interest payments and freeing up money that previously went to the "oligarchs." This is my term for the large creditors who delight in keeping us in their debt and financial slavery.

You may have discovered by now that the reason you were so much in debt in the first place was due to large recurring interest payments in addition to uncontrolled spending.

After the pain is over, you will enjoy spending your money in freedom. Now you need to hold firmly to purchasing for cash, except for large investment purchases such as a house. You can save to buy a car or purchase an inexpensive car and work your way up.

> After the pain is over, you will enjoy spending your money in freedom.

Personal Comments

When I was using credit, I bought a new car about every two years. Now I buy pre-owned cars privately or at auction. This for me is a change of mindset. For most of my adult life, I had a bank loan owed on a car. For the past several years, we have lived debt free, except for our house mortgage and a business loan. We can decide what to buy and when to make purchaseswith cash only. If we can't buy it with cash, we can't afford it. As I mentioned above, we use Visa/debit card and prepaid credit card only.

Spending on Large Purchases

In addition to credit card debt, people make two purchases that are potentially destructive to their finances. These are car and house purchases.

1. Car Purchase. A car is considered a depreciating asset. If you get a large auto loan for a new car, you have just placed a heavy burden on your budget. The value drops like a rock the moment you take it out of the dealership. It depreciates much faster than the average monthly payments. You may not feel the pain until you are ready to sell or when the warranty expires.

Ted Carroll tells the tale of Luckless Luke and Knowledgeable Kevin. Luke saw an ad for a new car. He checked it out and got excited. He pays $199 per month at 7.5 percent interest. After sixty months of payments he has paid $12,139 for a $9,000 purchase value. Kevin buys a used car for cash. Like Luke, he paid the same $199 per month, but it goes to his investment account, which yields 8 percent annually. After sixty months Kevin has $15,130. He buys the same new car for cash with money left in his investment account.[93]

2. House Purchase. Houses often appreciate in value. Be careful with this investment since the housing market goes up and down.

Scenario 1

Two couples purchase their first home at about the same time. Both couples earn $80,000 annually. They each make a down payment of $20,000 plus closing costs. Both can obtain a $200,000 mortgage. The first couple takes the $200,000 mortgage for thirty years. The second couple buys a fixer-upper for $120,000 and makes the same payments as the first couple. Five years later the second couple sells the house and buys one across the street from the first couple for $240,000. Five years later, i.e., ten years since they bought their first house, two different scenarios are taking place in the homes across the street from each other. The first couple is looking at bills and twenty more years of mortgage payments. The second couple is breaking open a bottle of champagne and burning their mortgage.[94]

Scenario 2

You can pay off your mortgage several years early. Now that you are getting out of debt, you can afford to pay more on your mortgage. There are different ways to do this. One way is to keep your mortgage at the present rate and find out from your lender the payments you need to make to pay off your mortgage in the time of you're choosing. Then make the payments required to meet your new goal. The advantage is that if you change your mind later you just revert to the previous payment schedule.

Scenario 3

Another method I learned recently is to make the next month's payment with your current payment. For example, if you are making January's payment, include February's payment as well. The next month you will be making the March payment. You may include April's payment. Make sure to indicate to your lender what the payment is for. Keep a careful record as the payments are skipped

---

93 Ted Carroll, *Live Debt Free*, p. 49.
94 Ted Carroll, *Live Debt Free.*, pp. 15ff.

so you know which month you are paying on. Keep indicating to the lender in writing when you make your payments which months you are paying. Doing it this way gives you the flexibility to revert to your original payment without penalty. Bear in mind if you paid for the current month of January and you paid for February as well, the next time you will be paying for March and April, then May and June. This should be clearly marked on the payment slip.

Yet another way is to pay your mortgage biweekly rather than monthly. In that way, you will add four extra payments for the year. That will take several years off the length of your mortgage.

When you are debt free you will have discretionary funds to spend as you like and help charities and needy causes. Church members will be able to tithe and assist with church projects without the added stress of running out of funds. You will be able to help family members.

Do you control your life or do your creditors?

It's all in the mindset. One makes a paradigm shift from living on borrowed money with stifling interest payments to living with a debt-free mindset. The process leading to financial freedom may be challenging at first but it gets easier as you get used to the strategies.

> One makes a paradigm shift from living on borrowed money with stifling interest payments to living with a debt-free mindset.

Remember: You cannot force your spouse or anyone else to live debt free, you can free only yourself. Once you understand the strategies of debt-free living, you may share them with your spouse with the hope of getting him/her on board. But action is indispensable.

"Even if you're on the right track you'll get run over if you just sit there." Will Rogers.

So, let's get started on the way to financial freedom.

Chapter Nine

Sex & Intimacy

Preview

The love that is thoughtful and unselfish makes life's greatest dream come to pass, but sex without love can make of life a horrible nightmare.[95]

You can certainly have fun without romance, but it's nearly impossible to have romance without fun. In The Sex-Starved Marriage, Michele Davis related this frustrating experience:

> Please, please help me. I am going through hell!! I am twenty-eight years old, married with a three-year-old daughter. For the past three years, my wife has avoided being sexual with me. It has slowly gone from having sex maybe twice a week to now, if I'm lucky, once a month. And even then, it's not really having sex. There is no foreplay. She doesn't even kiss me.
>
> I get completely angered, hurt, and resentful towards her because I can't understand how she could be so cruel to me. I want to be there when my little girl wakes up in the morning and goes to bed at night. But I also don't want to be with a woman who doesn't want to be with me.
>
> So I struggle every day with what I should do because I can't keep living like this. I'm miserable.[96]

This book was written for the purpose of helping people in this young man's situation. This chapter on sex and intimacy should point the sincere seeker in the right direction.

---

95 S. I. McMillen, "The Superlatives of Sex," *The Marriage Affair*, p. 382.
96 Michelle Weiner Davis, *The Sex-Starved Marriage*, pp. 1ff.

Combining a recent Redbook magazine survey of some 10,000 respondents with expert advice from "top sex experts," Pamela Lister and other Redbook editors produced a book entitled Married Sex, which offers revealing opinions on current attitudes to sex by married couples in America. Surprisingly enough, the research concludes that more than half the men and women say they desire their spouse as much today as when they got together. One-fifth desires their spouse even more. That is positive news for the embattled marriage in our society.

When asked how much they desire their spouse compared to when they got married, the "As Much" category was 57 percent for men and 55 percent for women. Unfortunately, 21 percent of both males and females confessed that they had grown apart.[97]

From the outset, let me state univocally that I reject the glamorous ideal of sex that Hollywood has foisted upon us during the past several decades. I mean the kind where two strangers meet and within minutes they are in bed together. When the sex is over one will turn to the other and ask, "By the way, what is your name?" This chapter will not focus on the titillating aspects of sex. It will emphasize how to improve sexual experience within marriage.

We will review the subject of sex in the context of marital intimacy. I reject the notion that sex is to be performed only for physical pleasure. Because sex is pleasurable and sexual desire is insatiable, sex can become an end in itself. A constant search for sexual satisfaction as biology dictates is an unfortunate use of sex. Considering the intimacy of the sex act, I can't understand how people could give their bodies in such an intimate way to a stranger or to someone with whom they have no meaningful relationship.

Personal Story

During my mid-teen years, I attended a boys' public secondary boarding school. Peer pressure was enormous. The adventurous boys left campus on the weekends to visit girls in the nearby towns. During the following days they told their adventurous tales. I was very curious about their sexual exploits but never ventured out to share their experience. I suppose my upbringing had a profound influence on me. Sometime between high school and college I developed my own philosophy of life and couched it in a few brief words:

"The decision of a moment can change the destiny of a lifetime."

Those words have guided my life ever since those formative years. My view of sexual activity has been certainly influenced by that philosophy. For that reason I waited until marriage to become sexually involved and I am doggedly

---

97 Pamela Lister, *Married Sex*, p. 13.

determined to keep sex within marriage only. I don't believe in excuses or hypocrisy. Loyalty to the marriage vow should not be compromised.

Another decision I made during my teens also helped me to avoid moral capitulation. I observed that one or more of three problems crippled many great men in history: unrestrained quest for power, love of money, and illicit sex. At age eighteen, I decided to avoid them regardless of the temptation. In my book, Making Marriage Meaningful, I related how I was tempted to surrender this principle in the area of sex twice in my career. I avoided failure by the grace of God and my earlier commitment. I can assure you that my wife is gracious, loving, and forgiving, but not on that issue. Regarding unfaithfulness in sex, I believe that for Pam it's one strike and you're out. Perhaps, Petula may be more merciful. Over the years I have found that many of my ideas about sex and intimacy were wrong or inaccurate. Much of this knowledge came from other boys during my high school and college years, misleading information on television, and inaccurate ideas in reading materials intended for entertainment rather than conveying accurate information about sex. After getting married, I was forced to revise some of my views. But others continue to change over the years. During my research and writing, I had to accelerate the changes. Much of what I have learned caused me to think that many people who are married for several years, even decades, still lack some of the basic strategies and information necessary to Develop an intimate and meaningful relationship with their spouses.

Problem

Sandra Leiblum and Judith Sachs described well the problem many people have with sex.

> Sex comes with a big shiny bow wrapped around it: a present that
> promises the ultimate physical, mental, emotional, and spiritual
> fulfillment, but once the box is open, everything's in pieces and
> there are no instructions.[98]

Despite the effort of the commercial and entertainment industries to saturate the society with immoral sexual images and sexually perverted attitudes, the discussion of sex in many circles in our society still remains fairly conservative. Many Christian and morally sensitive individuals do not readily discuss sex openly with their spouses and their children. Adding to the problem of limited correct knowledge about sex

---

98 Sandra Leiblum and Judith Sachs, *Getting The Sex You Want*, p. 2.

is the avalanche of false information about sex that permeates our society. The effect is that we feel overwhelmed with too much information about sex while we suffer a serious lack of quality information to build successful marital and family relationships.

> We feel overwhelmed with too much information about sex while we suffer a serious lack of quality information to build successful marital and family relationships.

The bottom line is that the real issues are not discussed. Sex does not only give pleasure. It brings its share of problems, too. Dr. David Schnarch, in a recent book about resolving sexual problems, focused on some studies that revealed that about 35 percent of men in the United States, ages forty to seventy, had sexual arousal difficulties. That represents approximately twenty to thirty million men. A New England Journal of Medicine study of normal couples discovered that:

> Forty-eight percent of women had difficulty getting excited and 33 percent had difficulty staying excited. While these results are striking, also consider this: 86 percent of these women said their sexual relationship was satisfying, and only 15 percent of their husbands knew their wives had problems![99]

> The bottom line is that the real issues are not discussed. Sex does not only give pleasure. It brings its share of problems too.

Dr. David Schnarch further states:
> Other research suggests that the incidence of low sexual desire among women is closer to 50 percent. Sexual desire problems are among couples' most frequent sexual complaints.[100]

Because the main source of our knowledge about sex and relationships come from the Internet, movies, friends, novels, synopses from other people's relationships, and other unreliable sources, some people transfer this type of negative influence into their marriage. This results in unrealistic expectations and even ignorance about their spouse, sex, and the marriage itself. *The Healthy Marriage Handbook* puts it this way:

---

99 David Schnarch, *Resurrecting Sex*, pp. 50, 51
100 David Schnarch, Ibid., p. 50.

> Most women don't realize that testosterone creates a physiological drive in their husbands that demands expression every few days…women experience little physical drive for sexual release. Rather, they desire the relational closeness that leads to sexual intimacy.
>
> Many husbands assume their wives will get aroused and reach a climax as quickly as they do. But most women are only in the early arousal stage when their husbands have their orgasm. This discrepancy often leaves a woman feeling cheated when her husband falls asleep just when she's getting interested. And her husband ends up feeling inadequate as a lover since he has failed to bring his wife to orgasm.[101]

Sex therapists such as Dr. David Schnarch can testify to the fact that sexual unhappiness is widespread. They are aware that sexual dysfunctions and dissatisfactions are rampant among even normal, healthy couples.

Even in today's permissive society, people are hesitant to discuss their sex lives. Most likely the studies which attempt to obtain statistics regarding sexual attitudes may be understating the facts. A 1992 National Health and Social Life Survey study of a large sample of men and women between the ages of eighteen to fifty-nine revealed that 43 percent of women and 31 percent of men had a sexual problem during the previous year. It is obvious that if nearly one in two women and one in three men are having some sexual difficulties, there is a real secret problem in many bedrooms at night.

However, a significant number of couples having sexual difficulties can receive help by taking a hard look at their attitude to life in general, their attitude toward their spouse, and their attitude to sex.

We will not take the time to explore all the many reasons for sexual problems. In fact, some arise from medical reasons. Couples should seek advice from trained experts in medicine and sex therapy. However, a significant number of couples having sexual difficulties can receive help by taking a hard look at their attitudes to life in general, their attitudes toward their spouse, and their attitudes to sex. The information in this chapter should serve to help couples with problems they can resolve without medical intervention.

---

101 Louise A. Ferrebee, Gen. Editor, *The Healthy Marriage Handbook*, pp. 85, 86.

Paradigm Nine:
The Law of Diminishing Returns

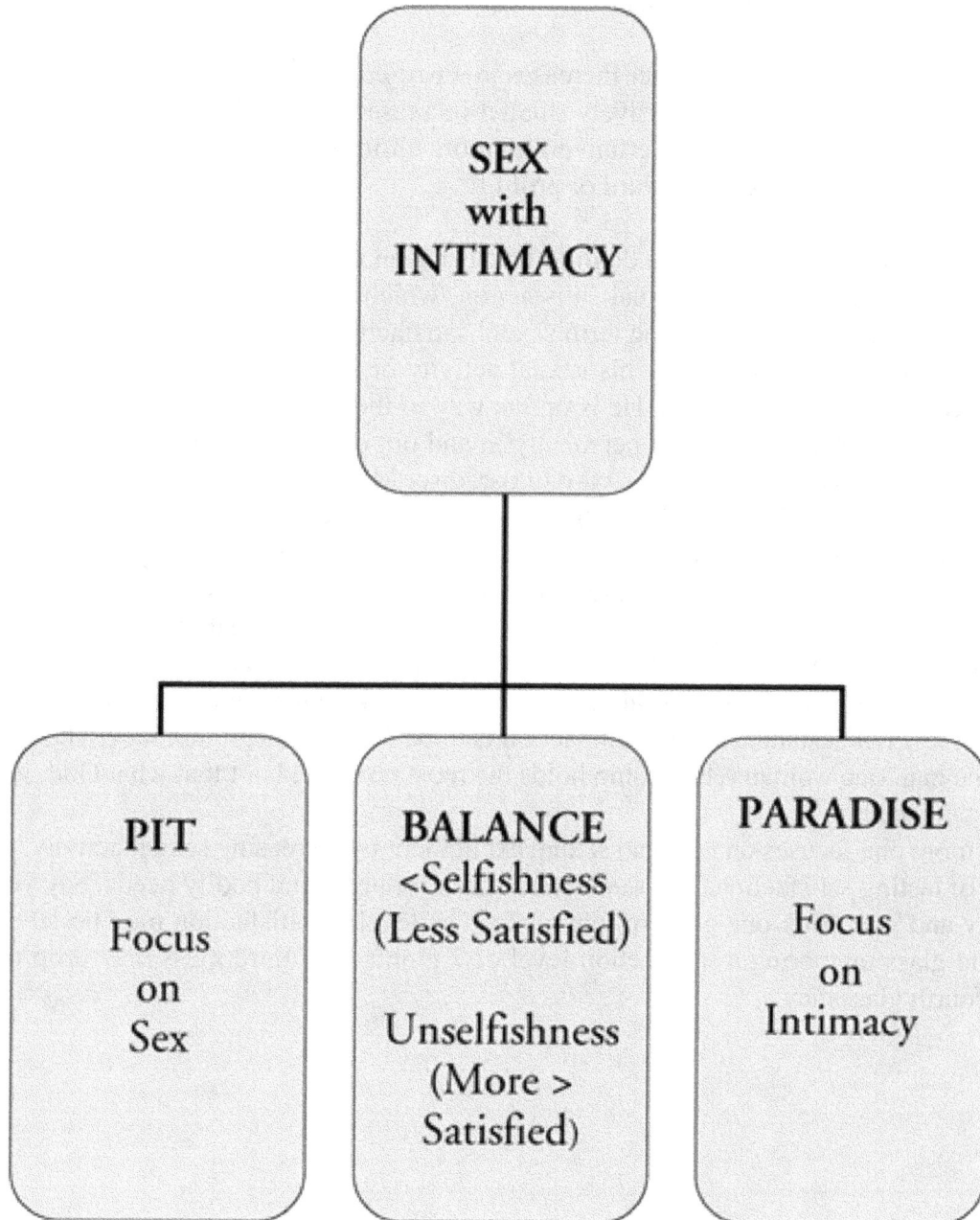

**SEX
with
INTIMACY**

PIT

Focus
on
Sex

BALANCE
<Selfishness
(Less Satisfied)

Unselfishness
(More >
Satisfied)

PARADISE

Focus
on
Intimacy

> The highest level of sustained sexual satisfaction is to be found through intimacy.

Paradigm Nine Explained

The Law of Diminishing Returns is a principle in economics which states:

> After a certain point, further increases in a particular factor of
> production lead to progressively smaller increases in output.
> The idea [is] that, after a certain point, more effort or investment
> in a project brings less reward or profit.[102]

Paradigm Nine aims to show a definite link between ongoing pleasurable sex and intimacy. When a man seeks his own sexual satisfaction, which is often the case, he will most likely lessen his chances of gaining long term sexual satisfaction in his relationship. If he focuses on sexual satisfaction by increasing his sexual activity or sexual deviancy, he will reach a point of increasingly less satisfaction. He is on his way to the pit. However, by focusing on intimacy, seeking to satisfy his partner personally in and out of bed, he is more likely to enjoy great sex for the long term. He is on his way to paradise. Many people are balancing in the middle between sexual satisfaction and dissatisfaction until they begin to drift to the left toward the pit or develop strategies for intimacy and move toward the right and discovering lasting pleasure.

I can see a striking application of the theory of diminishing returns to sex. Those in our society who are focused on sexual pleasure for its own sake try to convince their unsuspecting audience that more sex leads to more satisfaction and unlimited sex leads to unlimited pleasure. This attitude certainly results in sexual aberration, sexual deviancy, and personal frustration. The highest level of sustained sexual satisfaction is to be found through intimacy. That's the reason the one man/one woman relationship holds the most promise. Isn't that what God, who created us, established?

The more one focuses on personal sexual excitement by increasing sexual activity, the less the level of lasting satisfaction. The same is true of other urges and bodily needs. Say you are very thirsty and you drink one glass of lemonade. The level of satisfaction may be 10 points. The second glass may bring a satisfaction level of 7 points. The third glass may drop to 2 points. The fourth glass may

---

102 *The Tormont Webster's Illustrated Encyclopedic Dictionary.*

result in dissatisfaction or a minus 2 points, and so on. The fourth glass of lemonade may even be better quality, more delicious, more refreshing but not for the person who just had three glasses. What is more, too much of a good thing could be harmful if not dealt with wisely. The more one focuses on personal sexual excitement by increasing sexual activity, the less the level of lasting satisfaction.

Providing Solutions

Let's take a look at sex within the marriage relationship.

Attitude to Sex

After reminding us that for a man the emotion of love culminates in sexual union and for a woman love finds its fulfillment in intimacy and security in the relationship, Dr. David Mace, a marriage counselor, makes this observation:

> I know that a great many married people could be happier together if they were more fully aware of this difference between men and women. Mishandled, it can certainly wreck marriages. Rightly managed, it enriches rather than estranges. The husband is able to draw from his wife a sexual response, which enables her to value their physical intimacy as much as he does. At the same time his wife, through her own outgoing love, is able to kindle in her husband an affection and gratitude which make him eager to please her at every possible opportunity. And that is a description of a happy marriage[103]

> For the man the emotion on love culminates in sexual union and for a woman love finds its fulfillment in intimacy and security in the relationship.

What I would like to reinforce at this point is that sex is a vital part of a successful marital relationship. Dr. David Mace has made it plain that sexual response is intricately bound up with couples' relationships. Troubled marriages usually experience a breakdown in meaningful sexual relations.

---

103 David Mace, "The Art of Married Love," *The Marriage Affair*, p. 378.

Remember that for a man the emotion of love culminates in sexual union. If that climax is denied him the whole process is brought to a standstill. The wife who doesn't understand this can easily wreck her marriage. That is why some wonderful women make a complete muddle of things and then are at a loss to know what went wrong.[104]

I was not surprised to learn from Redbook's survey that "a whopping 68 percent of men crave more, no matter how much they are getting now!"[105] Women are not saying they want less, since 55 percent say they are satisfied, but by comparison only 40 percent say they want more. Both spouses need to take into account the gender differences in relation to sexual satisfaction. We would expect that the women's movement of the 1970s and 1980s would cause women to be bolder in initiating sex. Yet two-thirds of men in the survey say they wish their wives would initiate sex more often.

Denial of Sex

Some husbands and wives use sex as a weapon, a means of punishing their mate. This is a sure way to break down the sacred bond between two partners. If they have a quarrel, the issue should be dealt with without resorting to with holding sex. Otherwise, a new problem is inadvertently introduced into the relationship. This time it could lead to hostility because sex is an emotionally charged issue. As several marriage counselors attest, men gain intimacy through sex. They then respond to their wives with affection which women need. Those who are acquainted with God's counsels in the Bible will recall his charge:

> The husband should give to his wife her conjugal rights [sexual rights], and likewise the wife to her husband. For the wife does not rule over her own body, but the husband does; likewise the husband does not rule over his own body, but the wife does. Do not refuse one another except perhaps by agreement for a season.[106]

Some Christians mask their reluctance to have a healthy sexual relationship with within marriage under the cloak of spirituality. Surely, we should have a deep spiritual life but we should not use that to deny our spouse the sexual response they deserve and expect.

---

104 David Mace, Ibid., p. 378.
105 Pamela Lister, *Married Sex*, p. 19.
106 1 Corinthians, *Chapter* 7: 3-5.

In an article in Redbook entitled "Sex Secrets of Really Happy Couples," written by Lisa Lombardi, the fourth of ten counsel's cautions?

They never withhold nooky as punishment. Warning: 'Expressing anger by never being in the mood will doom your sex life,' says [Dr. Tina] Tessina. Why? Besides the fact that it turns what should be a loving and giving act into a commodity, once sex becomes part of a couple's power struggle, so much resentment builds that soon neither partner wants sex. So instead of feigning fatigue or rolling away from your guy next time you're annoyed, speak up and clear the air without sex being on the table.[107]

Dr. Tina Tessina suggests further that couples who participate in makeup sex have an emotional advantage since they keep up intimacy during tough times, which contributes to making love last.[108] However, I would suggest to couples that before attempting to engage in sex after a conflict, they should have an intimate dialogue to resolve the problem. This approach may prove to be more therapeutic and lasting. When sex precedes a serious attempt to resolve, or at least clarify, the irritating issue, one or both partners may feel used. In addition, the problem may only be masked rather than be resolved.

Sexual Problems

Let's take a look at a few of the problems that affect a healthy sexual relationship in marriage.

Sex and Anxiety

Anxiety and stereotypes may inhibit a healthy sexual relationship. There are many sources of anxiety: the stereotype of old age, tiredness, conflict with spouse, religious stereotypes, health problems, the feeling that you will not perform to the satisfaction of your partner, the fear of premature ejaculation, elicit affairs, guilt, life's problems such as financial problems, and many more.

Sex and Aging

Ample research findings debunk the theory that sex declines significantly with age. I grew up hearing and believing that false view. Those who believe that may

107 Lisa Lombardi "Sex Secrets of Really Happy Couples," *Redbook*, March 2005, p. 162.
108 Lisa Lombardi, Ibid., p. 162.

fulfill their own prophecy by decreasing their desire for sex as they grow older. They may not want to bother or simply feel that they have outgrown sex. The dirty old man syndrome may also produce negative feelings. The study done by Samuel and Cynthia Janus and published in The Janus Report in 1993 has changed many of our attitudes to sex, at least indirectly. In the category of sexual frequency from daily to weekly, the frequency of over sixty-five-year-olds was men 69 percent and women 74 percent. The eighteen-to-twenty-six-year-old category was men 72 percent and women 68 percent. Sexual frequency was remarkably equal for both groups.[109] Perhaps the Januses interviewed mainly healthy subjects. However, other surveys have supported these findings. Most married couples have sex an average of one to three times per week.

> Many studies have shown that sex is normal for couples until late in life.

The desire for sex is different from the need or ability to participate in sex. But age alone should not prevent men or women from having sex. Many studies have shown that sex is normal for couples until late in life. However, changes occur emotionally and physiologically which necessitate adjustments both for the individual and for the couple. In other words, it won't be "business as usual." When we get older significant changes occur in our bodies.

When my wife reached menopause, I observed with a sense of helplessness as she had to cope with unpredictable changes in her body and often in her mood. I was taken by surprise since I had only limited theoretical understanding of the subject and, after all, I didn't think that menopause concerned me. But it did when it occurred. I was face to face with a world of changes.

I have said jokingly to Pam that I have had two wives in one. The one I married was very slim and the other is just right. I hasten to add that I love both. Interestingly enough, after the storm came the calm. Pam is almost back to her former self in many respects. Sometimes I thought I had lost her interest because I didn't have sufficient patience and understanding to relate to her sensitively enough. Pam was not the only one changing. I was, too. Despite the emotional storms and calms, our love and commitment endured. Now we are closer than before the turbulent changes began, thanks to her patience and my growth!

Marriage professionals have pointed out that as we grow older we need to make adjustments to cope with the changes in each other. If not, couples inevitably grow apart and end up merely tolerating each other or getting divorced.

---

109 Samuel and Cynthia Janus, *The Janus Report*, p. 21.

Many couples seem to think that just as they can't slow down the human aging process, they can't do anything to alter the aging process of marriage. They let the relationship take its 'normal course' by happenstance until it threatens to break down, and by then it may be too late.[110]

One of the many considerations for older couples is that hormones do not flow in torrents as they did when they were younger. Because their bodies don't respond readily to sex, they may begin to think that the game is over. But that's when a new phase is beginning. It could prove to be less fiery but deeper and more meaningful. Arousal may take longer as your body responds more slowly. Now is the time to accept reality. Both partners need to accept each other as they are and not as they expect them to be. They should accept themselves as they discover the changes that inevitably occur. For some people these lessons are hard to learn. The result is constant friction with their spouses. It's like shouting at the rain when you want to see the sunshine. Dr. Willard F. Harley Jr. writes:

While sexual problems cause tension and unhappiness in many marriages these difficulties can be solved more easily than one might think. In most cases it requires education. To deal with such problems, the couple willing to learn what they need to know and to practice it together will achieve fulfillment.[111]

Dr. Steve Brody and Cathy Brody counsel:

But as the second half of life takes on new meaning physically, psychologically, and spiritually, it truly can be a time of sexual renewal, deeper intimacy, and emotional flowering. There are pearls in this supposed dustbin, if you know where to look and how to search for them. Bright among them is the increased ease and comfort you can find with your partner and your body as you explore a new and more satisfying dimension to your sexual relationship.[112]

110 Judith S. Wallerstein and Sandra Blakelee, *The Good Marriage*, p. 269.
111 Willard F. Harley, *His Needs, Her Needs*, p. 52.
112 Steve and Cathy Brody, *Renew Your Marriage at Midlife*, p. 184.

Sex and Health

There is a direct relationship between sexual relationship and health. Since different people react differently to physical and psychological stimuli, it is obvious that all of us will not respond the same way to pressures, illnesses, or frustration. Some manage better than others. Nevertheless, when our bodies are ill or we are under undue stress, most people will be unable to perform sexually. This is particularly true of women. That is amply demonstrated during the time when children are young and need much attention. The amount of time and energy mothers' utilize usually leaves them drained and unable to participate freely in sex frequently.

> There is a direct relationship between sexual relationship and health.

One writer expresses the problem this way:

> Ultimately, you can't have truly great sex if you don't know how to cultivate intimacy with a partner. Nor can you have great sex if your attitudes, your health, your life are in disarray.[113]

Dr. Eric Rimm, associate professor at the Harvard School of Public Health, postulated that lack of potency may precede a heart attack. He explains:

> Being a vigorous exerciser and adding other healthy lifestyles factors such as not smoking, staying lean, and drinking only moderately had the effect of adding ten years to a man's sexual status. Exercise seems to benefit the small arteries that control erections, much as exercise benefits other arteries, such as those that feed the heart. Thus what happens to the penis may be an early warning of what could happen to the heart, such as a heart attack.[114]

Tiredness

Although it is common for spouses to decline sex with their partners using the excuse of being tired, perhaps we have underestimated the true effect of tiredness on not only desire but ability to perform normally during sexual activity.

---

113 See: Neil Wertheimer, Introduction to Stephen George et al., *A Lifetime of Great Sex.*
114 *The Paducah Sun, Kentucky*, August 25, 2003, p. 13A.

Unfortunately, our fast-paced society causes not only occasional tiredness but chronic tiredness as well.

Consequently, many people don't have enough energy to complete their normal day's chores after work. That accounts for so many people who try unsuccessfully to maintain an exercise program, spend quality time with their children, and pay proper attention to their spouses. Being drained physically may also contribute to short tempers, anger, and harsh words, thereby reducing the level of intimacy needed for pleasurable sex.

Personal Story

During my late thirties, my exceedingly heavy work load contributed directly to my lack of ability to perform satisfactorily during sex. My wife, though patient and understanding, was subjected to some difficult experiences during that time. I was convinced that age had caught up with me. I believed I just needed to accept the inevitable. But that was not the case. Tiredness was the cruel culprit. Sometime after that problem began, I took a leave of absence to return to uni- versity. Not long after I started my new program, the problem disappeared and never returned. With the change of pace, my body had time to renew its energy. Later, during meno- pause when my wife faced her challenging times and I had difficulty understanding her mood, she calmly reminded me of my trying times during my late thirties. Attention should be given to proper rest in order to enhance health as well as foster normal sexual functioning.

Intimacy is the unreserved sharing of a couple's thoughts, desires, dreams, goals, fears, deep inner feelings, and, in essence, themselves with one another.

Intimacy

The sexual act is a very intimate experience. To try to experience sex without intimacy as our modern culture encourages may well lead to a few moments of pleasure, but in the end it will lead to a lifetime of regrets and emptiness. For a long time, I struggled with the desire to understand whether sex was only intended for procreation or if it had another significant purpose as well. Recently, I solved that puzzle. I realized that God in his wisdom recognized our need for intimacy as we live our lives with one partner.

> To try to experience sex without intimacy as our modern culture
> encourages may well lead to a few moments of pleasure but in the end
> it will lead to a lifetime of regrets and emptiness.

Sex provides the unique means to achieve and maintain an intimate bond with our spouse. It is a lifelong quest to achieve deep relationship through intimacy rather than occasional flight of ecstasy. Those who follow the modern trend of doing what feels well rather than what is good will eventually discover, perhaps too late, they have lost the essence of the lasting pleasure they sought to achieve. For instance, when a woman discovers that all a man wants from her is sex, how enduring can that relationship become? There is much, much more to sex than the physical act. The glamorous images which Hollywood and our permissive society portray are misleading and shallow. Let's explore the true meaning of intimacy and how we can achieve it.

Webster's Dictionary includes sexual intercourse as one of its definitions of intimacy. We frequently use these terms interchangeably. However, they are very different concepts or activities. There can be an intimate relationship without sex and a sexual relationship without intimacy. Our culture promotes the latter. But a successful marriage must have both. Intimacy is the unreserved sharing of a couple's thoughts, desires, dreams, goals, fears, deep inner feelings, and, in essence, of themselves with one another. In marriage, intimacy is unlike any other relation- ship. It is a total giving of the marriage partners to each other emotionally, mentally, spiritually, and physically for life. A significant part of intimacy is taking care of each other's needs lovingly.

Sex is an area of potential conflict. Frequently, the pressures from everyday issues result in the abandonment of intimacy. When that occurs, sex becomes routine and even resented, especially by the wife.

Diane Rehms, a nationally syndicated Public Radio broadcaster, and her husband, John Rehms, a prominent attorney, explain how their effort to resolve their problems with sex failed. After forty-two years of marriage, they reflect on their experiences together. Both explain how the mundane issues of life cooled their passion for closeness. John explains:

> [M]aking love often became a psychological weapon, wielded in marital
> skirmishes and even war. Withholding it was a form of retaliation for
> the infliction of real or imagined wounds. Restoring it after a period of
> destructive silence was an awkward means of expressing regret.
> Demanding it as a form of release disregarded Diane's feelings and wishes.

In short making love became problematic. At times its presence
offered a means of reconciliation, when other avenues were cut off.
At other times, its absence exacerbated the tensions between us.[115]

John describes his compartmentalization as "romantic illusion." It's just like going away to an island. He conceived of using sex to transcend the problems in their marriage. He tried it and failed. He used sex for power in negotiating or retaliating, i.e., by withholding sex, seeking forgiveness, or reconnecting. That approach "boomeranged."

Diane explains why:

I have such a different feeling. As a woman, for me the sexual
encounter is very much an extension of the emotional encounter.
Time and time again, when we have been distant or isolated
from each other, you have approached sexually as a way to move
beyond the problem. But I am still in the problem and therefore
can't move that quickly from emotional feelings I am experiencing,
turn them off, and move toward becoming a sexual partner.[116]

Perhaps the greatest threat to achieving and maintaining intimacy is selfishness. As human beings, we are basically selfish. We express that daily through self-preservation. In marriage, though, we must think constantly about the well-being of our partner. We should seek to avoid that which he/she dislikes and strive to provide that which will please our partner. When we learn that lesson, marriage becomes a lifelong joyful experience. Remember the golden rule? It is invaluable in marriage.

If Dr. David Mace is right when he writes "that the basic drive which impels a woman into marriage is the need for a secure and sustained love relationship,"[117] then unhappy is the man who does not provide it. Dr. Jean Baker Miller, in her *New York Times* best-selling book, *Toward a New Psychology of Women*, insisted that basically women are givers and men are doers. She explains that in psy- chotherapy women spend much more time talking about giving than men do. She wrote:

---

115 Diane and John Rehms, *Toward Commitment*, p. 30.
116 Diane and John Rehms, *Toward Commitment*, p. 54.
117 David Mace, "The Art of Married Love," *The Marriage Affair*, p. 376.

> They [women] frequently are upset if they feel they are not givers.
> They wonder what would happen if they were to stop giving, to even
> consider not giving? The idea is frightening and the consequences too
> dire to consider. By contrast, the question of whether he is a giver or
> giving enough does not enter into a man's self-image. Few men feel
> that giving is a primary issue in their struggles for identity.[118]

Dr. Jean Baker Miller wrote this in the seventies when women were struggling for equality in society. She has answered for me a question I long mulled over: "Why do women feel that they give men sex but few people see men as giving sex to women?" There is a basic lack in the sexual equation when this view is perpetuated without modification. Pam used Dr. Jean Baker Miller's book in one of her college courses during the late seventies. When I saw it and began reading the first few pages, it was fascinating to me. I observed the comments Pam wrote in the margins throughout the book. She must have learned a lot from it and her knowledge helped her to change while I was left in the dark for several more years. Here are a few samples. Pam wrote, "the integrated woman" beside such passages as:

> In a situation of inequality the woman is not encouraged to take her
> own needs seriously, to explore them, to try to act on them as a separate
> individual. She is enjoined from engaging all of her own resources and
> thereby prevented from developing some valid and reliable sense of her
> own worth. Instead, the woman is encouraged to concentrate on the needs
> and development of the man.[119]

She underlined ideas such as:

> It is true that women, like everyone, are motivated out of the
> wellsprings of their own being, and carried to its "perfection,"
> it produces the martyr syndrome or the smothering wife and
> mother.[120]

But what caught my attention most was her comment beside the idea that women were liberating themselves from being givers in sex. Pam wrote: "Concept getting outdated," beside this passage:

---

118 Jean Baker Miller, *Toward A Psychology of Women*, p. 49.
119 Jean Baker Miller, *Toward a New Psychology of Women*, p. 18.
120 Jean Baker Miller, Ibid., p. 61.

For the present it is of extreme importance to stress that women have been led to feel that they can integrate and use all their attributes if they use them for others, but not for themselves. They have developed the sense that their lives should be guided by the constant need to attune themselves to the wishes, desires, and needs of others.121[121]

Another comment is even more direct:

> To say that women believe they must serve others may seem a commonplace observation....[M]any people miss its overwhelming importance as a factor in creating problems for women...This happens when clinicians accept it as 'just part of the usual backdrop,' not realizing that many women truly cannot tolerate or allow themselves to feel that their life activities are for themselves.[122]

Pam wrote in the margin: "especially the sex-partner relationship problem."

Was I left out in the cold while all this change was taking place? I believe so. In retrospect, I think I felt the changes occurring and was forced to adapt or be doomed. The significant point here is that both partners must take an egalitarian approach to sex and other areas of relationship between them. Dr. Jean Baker Miller's observations are vital and contemporary. She explains:

> It is interesting to note that the new forms of therapy for sexual dysfunctions focus simultaneously on giving and on taking responsibility for one's own pleasure. That is, each person not only has to admit to her/his role as a giver, but also must accept her/his role as a receiver of pleasure.[123]

> The point of significance here is that both partners must take an egalitarian approach to sex and other areas of relationship between them.

---

121 Jean Baker Miller, Ibid., p. 60.
122 Jean Baker Miller, Ibid., p. 62.
123 Jean Baker Miller, Ibid., p. 50.

Keys to Successful Sex:

To have a successful marriage, it is vital for us to internalize the concept that sex in marriage should not be reduced to physical pleasure but linked to intimacy. The search for intimacy should always be primary. Women often feel that men are having sex with them without being intimate. When that occurs, the female partner will find it difficult to express intimacy. I have heard it said that some women fake expressions of pleasure to give the man a sense of satisfaction from pleasing her. Some men find it difficult to show deep intimacy without desiring sex. But both partners need to make an effort to express intimacy on an ongoing basis without expecting that sex will follow. Having fun together by touching, hugging, and kissing regularly encourages closeness and fosters intimacy. Similarly, effort should be made to include intimacy with sex.

Here is the best illustration I have found for describing how sex and intimacy are inseparably linked if couples want to achieve success in their relationship. It will be followed by a revealing description of how the process works for men and women.

Dr. Barbara DeAngelis, a marriage therapist, was counseling a couple who appeared to be heading for divorce. The wife didn't feel like having sex with her husband anymore. Her husband didn't seem to recognize the problem. He seemed bewildered as she explained her dilemma. After some time the therapist decided to interview her alone and, after some difficulty in discovering the real basis of their problem, she finally asked her to describe their last sexual encounter. After describing the event, she proceeded to rate the experience as a three on a scale of one to ten, with ten being the best.

In his wife's presence, the therapist quizzed her husband again. The therapist wondered why his wife was so angry with him since he seemed to be such a lovely and agreeable person. In her presence, Dr. DeAngelis asked him to describe the same sexual encounter with his wife and rate it on a scale from one to ten, ten being the highest. After describing the episode, he judged the experience a nine. Then he added: "I love this woman so much! I worship her! How could I be so lucky?" His wife, who was listening intently, broke down in tears, leaped from the couch and embraced him as she exclaimed, "That's a ten! That's a ten!"[124]

The problem between them was not lack of love but lack of intimacy. He was performing sex without sharing himself with her. He should have demonstrated to her that he needed her and not merely that he needed sex. He failed to let her feel that she was precious to him. Their bodies connected but not their spirits, their deep inner feelings. Since she did not feel the flow of affection from her

---

124 Barbara DeAngelis, *What Women Want Men to Know*, pp. 309-312

mate, sex became irritating. Similarly, if she had turned down his sexual advances, he would have felt rejected.

Dr. Barbara DeAngelis pointed out that whereas a woman needs only one key (physical) to un-lock a man's passions, a man needs two keys to open the door to her passions physical touch and intimacy. She explains that when you allow your wife to be love starved, you will be sex starved. When a man makes sexual advances to his wife, she processes her response through a system Dr. Barbara DeAngelis terms "Emotional Headquarters" in her brain, which serves as the "Supervisor of Sex and Intimacy." She writes:

> The Supervisor of Sex and Intimacy in the brain makes a decision—it's not a good night for this woman to have sex. Maybe in a few days if he is nicer to her. She decides not to send the sensory information on to the woman's body. That means no matter what the man does to try to get his wife aroused, she won't feel turned on.[125]

Many marriages have had problems because the couples fail to understand the difference between the way emotions work for men or women. The foregoing example shows the specific reason. The effort a man makes to keep love flowing to his wife by constant small attentions will flow through her heart and back to him.

> Many marriages have had problems because the couples fail to understand the difference between the way emotions work for men or women.

Sex vs. Intimacy

A popular view in our society is that the focus should be on sexual pleasure. When I began to study the subject of sex in earnest, I was amazed at the countless number of books, articles, guides, and sex toys available to the public. Sexual perversion is a main attraction on the Internet and in films. In fact, I heard recently about a movement in the United States educational system to promote masturbation or self-pleasure in the lower elementary grades. Some sex therapists even promote sex toys and sexual gymnastics as ways to solve sexual dysfunction and low sexual desire. In other words, they seek solutions through sensation. However, sex is empty without true intimacy.

---

125 Barbara DeAngelis, Ibid., p. 316.

Sexual Surrender

Our society popularizes the hedonistic view of sex, i.e., if it is pleasurable, it is good. This is a quest for pleasure without pain. It is similar to the desire to achieve victory in a battle without expecting loss, pain, or struggle. The popular culture pushes us to seek our pleasure from sexual sensations. This means that from childhood we expect sex to provide ongoing lifelong pleasures. When the pleasure we seek is less in reality than our expectations, we tend to try unconventional sexual avenues to gain the pleasure we expect and demand. But emotions cannot be sustained and the law of diminishing returns cannot be superseded. When we fail to reach the desired result, we may seek to blame someone or something or proceed into aberrant behavior. This approach of focusing on sexual sensations short-circuits genuine intimacy. Making the effort to develop true intimacy will do three things:

1.   It will increase your desire to develop a closer relationship with your spouse;
2.   It will avoid pressuring your spouse to conform to your desires;
3.   It will help you concentrate on your own growth and maturity.

As you grow personally as well as in the relationship, you will avoid the pitfall of low self-esteem, which requires constant affirmation from your spouse. You will also avoid subservience in the relationship since you will be able to better identify what your needs are and discover better ways to fill them. As you grow you will discover better ways to please your mate. A great marital relationship is grounded in a great intimate relationship, which in turn leads to a satisfying sexual relationship.

Dr. David Schnarch opposes what he terms "sensate sex." He promotes a concept called sexual crucible. He writes:

> Low sexual desire is no fun, but it does have a purpose. It's part of
> marriage's intricate people-growing machine: it invites you to stretch
> yourself and your relationship.[126]

He believes that the key to dealing with low sexual desire is to be found in relationship, not biology. It begins with self-knowledge and leads to your choice to make internal or external changes.

---

126 David Schnarch, *Passionate Marriage*, p. 153.

> A great marital relationship is grounded in a great intimate relationship, which in turn leads to a satisfying sexual relationship.

Marital Misery (Marital Affairs)

A Personal Episode

Can you believe this experience I had some years ago? A lovely lady suggested to me enticingly that she would be satisfied if she could be close to me only once. It would be to her like a fantasy fulfilled. What do you think my answer was? Although I was extremely surprised, I tried to conceal my feelings. I asked her if she thought the experience would be exciting for me. She said anxiously, "Oh yes."

Then I said calmly, "The difference between us is that anything I do that is exciting, I want to repeat, so I don't think it is a good idea to start."

I learned long ago that the desire for sex, like thirst, is insatiable over time. Emotion rises and falls constantly. Once you surrender your will to a pleasurable emotion, it becomes increasingly difficult to resist recurrence, whether the activity is morally right or wrong.

In *The Rules for Marriage*, Ellen Fein and Sherrie Schneider write quite emphatically that if a spouse commits sexual infidelity once, the marriage is over. They proclaim, "We believe that once a cheater, always a cheater."[127]

They do not encourage people who cheat on their spouse to divorce, but they state unequivocally that with that one act the marriage is beyond repair.

> Even if he never cheats again, how will you know? How can you trust him? That's the problem, you can't.[128]

This opinion is logical but lacks the long reach of love and forgiveness. Before we reach such a conclusion, several factors must be considered. Who revealed the problem? Is he/she genuinely repentant? Is his/her life transparent or secretive? Is he/she trustworthy in other matters? What is his/her past experience in relating to the opposite sex? Does he/she have the capacity to forgive? Do they rely on divine help in their marriage?

---

127 Ellen Fein and Sherrie Schneider, *The Rules for Marriage*, p. 162.
128 Ellen Fein and Sherrie Schneider, Ibid., p. 162.

There is no excuse for an affair. However, people do have affairs. They err in sexual matters as in other areas of life. Some people learn from their mistakes, others don't. But nagging, using the guilty spouse's error as a weapon to get even, or allowing the fact of the affair to build resentment against your spouse, will prove destructive to the marriage. If the innocent partner is not able to overcome the sexual failure of the spouse, negative feelings may turn inwards and lead to depression, insecurity, lack of trust, and a source of sabotage.

Sexual affairs are attractive to some people because they get pleasure from them without the burden of the problems that face married couples. It is difficult for even happily married couples to maintain the blush of first love. Yet many people enter marriage with that expectation. Some people get married without considering the long-term effect marriage will have on them and what will be required of them to maintain a lasting relationship. Therefore, when they have to struggle to keep intimacy alive, they feel the spouse has betrayed them. During the middle years of marriage meaningful sex may be crowded out and replaced by tiredness after work, life's stresses, the spouses' waning interest, and a thousand other factors.

> Sexual affairs are attractive to some people because they get pleasure from it without the burden of the problems that face married couples.

When someone comes along displaying an air of excitement, adventure, and caring, suddenly erotic love springs to life again. For the moment, the illicit lovers overlook the consequences, and the effort needed to deal with sex at home vanishes. Apparently, this pleasure comes without the pain. Dr. William Glasser states:

> The main impetus by far for both married men and women who
> engage in long-term affairs is the attempt to recapture the intimacy,
> sexual and personal, that they no longer find in marriage.[129]

Dr. William Glasser points out that as long as people use external control psychology in their marriages, affairs will be more attractive. As soon as these "deadly habits" surface, the illicit affair ends.

---

129 William Glasser, *Getting Together and Staying Together*, p. 44.

For sex to be both desirable and successful, in or out of marriage, making love, not defending and attacking each other, has to be very much on the minds of both partners…[130]

I admire the thoughts expressed in Redbook's book Married Sex:

There's no question these are times of high expectation. At no other point have we demanded so much of marriage as an institution and of ourselves as life's partners: From one source, we seek romance, fun, shared values, emotional connection, economic parity, parental partnership, intellectual stimulation, physical attraction, sexual compatibility, erotic fulfillment…oh, and a good tennis partner. So, are we expecting too much? No. No, we are not. Every couple is entitled to establish the highest possible level of connection and to develop a bond that is primal, exciting, nurturing, and above all lasting. It's the highest form of human instinct to want to live in that secret place where we know we are perfect for each other, where our thrill for each is matched one to one.[131]

The biblical Solomon, the wise man, says: "Keep your heart with all vigilance; for from it flow the springs of life."[132]

---

130 William Glasser, Ibid., p. 45.
131 Pamela Lister, *Married Sex*, pp. 14, 15.
132 Proverbs, Chapter 4: 23.

Chapter Ten

Spirituality & Service

Preview

One day Robert Rainey, a great clergyman, was facing lots of criticism and misunderstanding. One of his friends said to him, "I just can't understand how you can endure it all and still seem to be so happy."

"Ah, but you see," said Rainey, "I am happy at home."

Let me borrow a metaphor about marriage I read some time ago. The ship of matrimony that God launched from the shores of the Garden of Eden has been caught in a cyclone of change. When the ship enters a raging storm, for every ten wedded couples in North America who embark on board for the journey, five will jump overboard and drown. Of the five couples remaining, three will have to be restrained on deck for various reasons other than happiness, such as children, fear of economic loss, or opposition to divorce. Only two couples are likely to feel happy and secure on board, despite the raging storm.

Can anything be done to save families? From a biblical perspective, the answer is a resounding "YES." God made us and he has given guidance in his word for our successful marital relationships. But are we paying attention?

My great concern is that the statistics I quoted above apply equally to professed Christian church members. Our task in this presentation is to discover biblical principles that should guide our families to develop successful relationships. However, we must take these principles seriously and apply them to our marriages.

Personal Story

I met my real girlfriend when I was nineteen years old. Recently out of high school, I was ready for the world, ready to experiment. Popular music fascinated me. Rock 'n Roll was just breaking on the music scene. The "juke box" in which you placed a few coins and selected your song was becoming a great fascination for young adults and teenagers. Little Richard, Elvis Presley, Laverne Baker, Fats Domino,

The Lyman Brothers, Bill Haley and His Comets, and Caribbean calypsos were only a few of the hit singers and musical styles that attracted me. I started to attend Saturday night dances and parties.

Having been brought up in a strict home during my teens, I did not get to engage in sex. I felt the time had come to explore that path. I had previously rejected smoking and alcohol as unwise habits. Providentially, as soon as I made the decision to venture out into the world of excitement and pleasure, I met Doug, a former schoolmate, who engaged me in a deep discussion about religion. We concluded that the best way to live our lives was to become Christians. It was certainly unusual for two young men, ages nineteen and twenty, to reason their way to that conclusion and embark upon such a new and challenging path without any prompting, pressure, or invitation. But we did! Since there were so many denominations all claiming to be the true religion, we felt unqualified to determine which to choose. After some discussion, we agreed to visit different churches to prove for ourselves which was closest to the biblical teachings.

On October 21, 1957, we met a Seventh-day Adventist layman who explained about the biblical Sabbath and the imminent return of Christ. We accepted Christ immediately and decided to be baptized and train for the ministry. I had to surrender my very first job as a bookkeeper at United Motors, an auto parts firm, because I refused to work on Saturdays, which I came to accept as the biblical Sabbath.

When I met Pam in February, 1959, I was just beginning to understand the demands of Christianity on my life as a teenager. Fortunately, since she was a settled Christian youth, we had no difficulty following the moral demands of our faith. We remained committed to our friendship for five years before getting married. But we never discussed or attempted to get involved with sex. In fact, I did not get my first kiss until after we were engaged to be married. That was four and one-half years after we met.

Pam and I were classmates in high school and college. We attended boarding schools together in two countries. We saw each other daily in classes, cafeteria, and at socials on weekends. But it never occurred to us to try any "hanky punky." We only held hands, admired each other, and talked, talked, talked.

Needless to say our marriage was founded on solid Christian principles which guided us and our four children over the years. Our religious faith taught us that sex before marriage is sinful and immoral, marriage is sacred, our bodies are the temples of God, and we should not defile our bodies with alcoholic beverages, caffeine, illicit drugs, unhealthy foods, and destructive lifestyles. We lived by those teachings and taught the same beliefs to our children.

Precious and I share similar religious convictions. We firmly believe in living in harmony with the teachings of the Bible. I believe God guided us to be married partners. Fortunately, we share our principles in seminars in bless others.

Problem

Christian families must face several issues. We cannot tackle them all in this chapter but here are a few significant ones: What is God's purpose for marriage? Does God sanction sex? If so, in what ways? Does God make allowances for male and female differences? Does he take into account our struggles with sexual drives? What is the biblical view of marriage and divorce? Is it wrong for a Christian to marry a non-Christian?

Not many decades ago, Canada and the United States of America were still entrenched in their heritage as mainly Christian nations. Several of the Ivy League universities and other prominent places of higher learning contributing to the pride of these nations were founded as religious-based institutions or were undergirded by biblical principles. Today, most of them have not only turned their backs on religious principles but vehemently oppose them. Harvard and Yale Universities in the U.S. and McGill and Toronto Universities in Canada are only a few of these institutions of higher learning, once religious based, now extremely secular and liberal.

I studied at McGill University in the mid-eighties and although I was in the religious history department, secularism and liberal theology were rampant. I know several capable conservative scholars who never survived to graduate. There was little room for conservative viewpoints. These scholars had to transfer to other universities. As a conservative Christian, I was fortunate to survive at McGill and graduate.

The liberalism on university campuses, the social revolution of the sixties and seventies, and the projection of free sex from Hollywood movie productions have combined to create a shift in the North American society from the traditional family structure to the lack of commitment to the traditional family that is so prevalent today. In about twelve years, 1966 to 1978, American society leaped from a 23 percent divorce rate to a 50 percent divorce rate. That rate has been surpassed in later decades. To add to the tragedy, since the Supreme Court sanctioned abortion, millions of innocent babies have never been given the opportunity to live outside of their mother's womb for even one day of the life God gave them. According to the Bible, marriage, sex, and life are sacred.

Dr. William J. Bennett, former national Education Secretary and now nationally syndicated talk show host, writes:

> Since 1960, fewer people are marrying, they are doing so later in life,
> they are having fewer children, they are spending less time with the
> children they do have, and they are divorcing much more frequently.
> Those who do not marry are having sexual relations at an earlier age

and contracting sexually transmitted diseases at much higher rates,
cohabiting in unprecedented numbers, and having a record number
of children out of wedlock. Finally, more children than ever before
live with only one parent.[133]

According to the U.S. Census Bureau, during the decade between 1990 and 2000, unmarried couples increased nearly 60 percent, from 3.2 million to 5.5 million. During the same period, the number of homes headed by single mothers versus those headed by homes with both mother and father increased nearly five times. Those who believe that the family structure provides the opportunity to build a safe and secure society mourn these numbers, but others cheer the destruction of the traditional family in our modern society.

---

133 William J. Bennett, *The Broken Hearth*, p. 14.

Paradigm Ten:
God's Design: Leadership and Influence

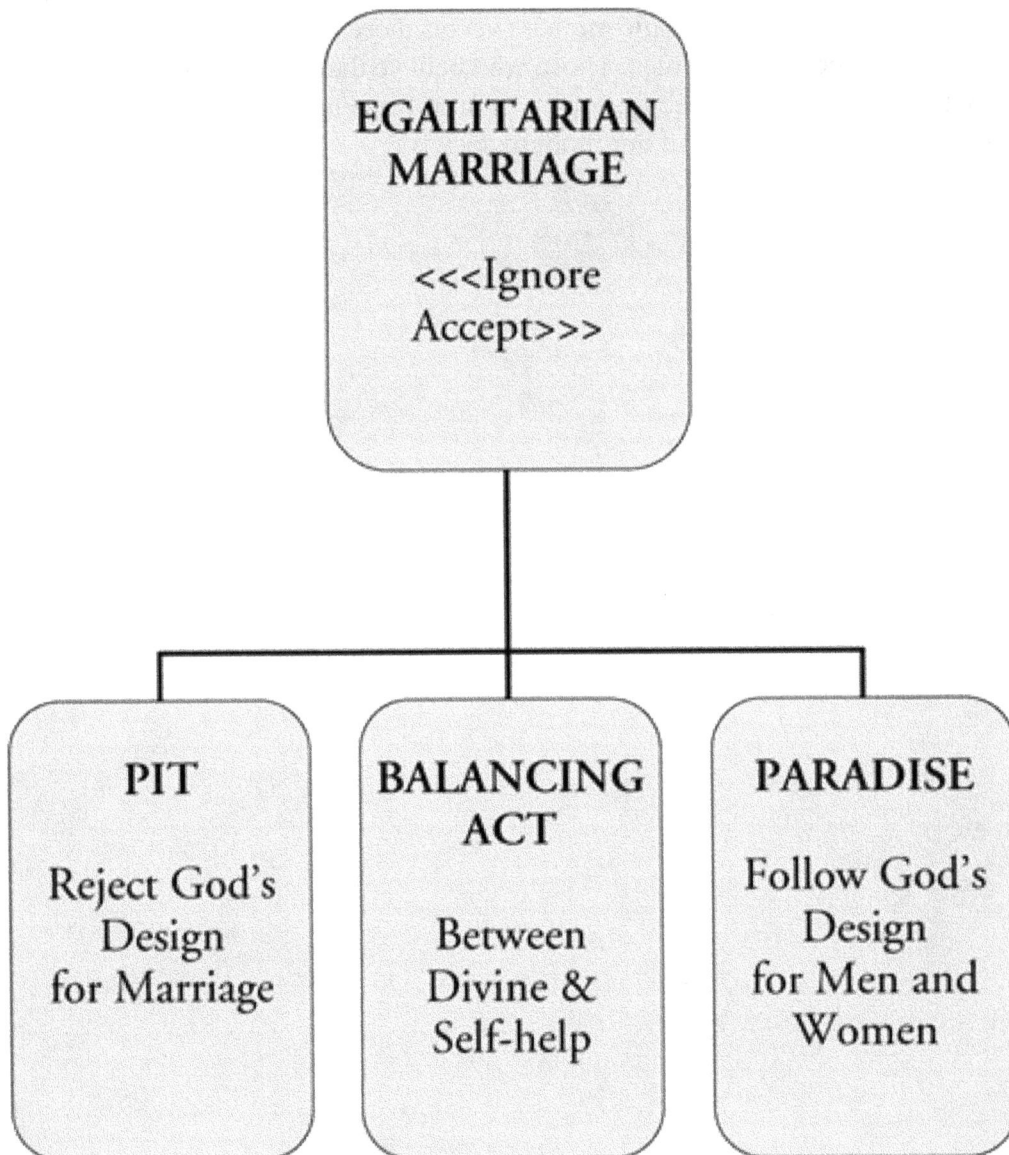

EGALITARIAN MARRIAGE

<<<Ignore
Accept>>>

PIT

Reject God's
Design
for Marriage

BALANCING ACT

Between
Divine &
Self-help

PARADISE

Follow God's
Design
for Men and
Women

Paradigm Ten Explained

Paradigm Ten helps us focus on the need to function within our God-given roles. The further we move from functioning within our design and hinder or discourage our spouse as he/she follows God's design, the closer we are to the pit of despair. The more we give support and recognition to our spouse as he/she functions within God's design, the closer we get to peace and paradise. It is just that simple. Husbands and wives who live in harmony honor their creator. If we try to balance between God's design and our own desire, we are not failing, but we are not enjoying the full pleasure that marriage offers.

Those who accept scriptural authority should not find it difficult to see God's plan for marriage. The Bible refers often to the marriage relationship. In Genesis, God created man and gave him authority over the creation. God gave him a wife to share his life as an equal. Adam said that the woman, Eve, was a part of himself, someone equal to himself created to shed her influence on his life.

God assigned to man the role of leadership and authority. He was created with strength to protect and provide. Eve was created to be his companion. Her role was to assist him and share his life. Notice that God made Eve with certain qualities different from Adam. A woman is graceful, charming, loving, and caring. That's how God made her. He prepared her to be a mother. Women possess a unique gift: to cradle and influence everyone born into the world. A woman's influence on a man is disarming and overpowering. She has built-in influence. Therefore, neither is better than the other. They complement each other. Both need each other to survive.

Providing Solutions

God Ordained Marriage

Most Christians are acquainted with the biblical story of creation in the book of Genesis. God created Adam and later took a rib from his side and formed Eve. In the first chapter of Genesis, the record indicates that God sanctioned their relationship as husband and wife.

> So God created man in His own image, male and female He created them. And God blessed them, and God said to them, "Be fruitful and multiply, and fill the earth, and subdue it."[134]

---

134 Genesis, Chapter 1:27, 28.

In Genesis chapter two, more information is added.

> Adam said, "This at last is bone of my bones and flesh of my flesh;
> she shall be called woman, because she was taken out of man."
> Therefore a man leaves his father and his mother and cleaves to his
> wife, and they become one flesh.[135]

We must conclude that God sanctioned marriage and established it as a sacred union between a man and a woman. Throughout the biblical record, there is strong evidence that God sought to preserve the sanctity of marriage. God declares:

> So take heed to yourselves, and let none be faithless to the wife of his
> youth. For I hate divorce, says the Lord.136[136]

Whereas in the Old Testament divorce was permitted for several reasons, even for trivial ones, Jesus made it clear that God intended that marriage should be permanent. When his questioners tried to get him to be flexible and agree with Moses' law permitting divorce for various reasons, Jesus replies:

> For your hardness of heart Moses allowed you to divorce your wives,
> but from the beginning it was not so. And I say unto you: whoever
> divorces his wife, except for unchastity [adultery], and marries another,
> commits adultery.137[137]

We should bear in mind that Jesus was responding to a specific issue regarding marriage. I don't believe he was giving a comprehensive view of the marriage relationship. For instance, what if a spouse abuses his/her mate in a life-threatening manner or sexually abuses their child? Are those actions to be condoned in a marriage relationship? Jesus made it clear that God established marriage as a permanent relationship. This is the ideal objective and should not be trivialized. However, Jesus clearly acknowledged that human limitations exit. Moses' law made allowances for the human condition that causes some people to fail to reach the ideal. The problem was that during the first century Jesus witnessed the breakdown of the vow

---

135 Genesis, Chapter 2:23, 24.
136 Malachi, Chapter 2:15, 16.
137 Matthew, Chapter 19:8, 9.

breakdown of the vow for trivial reasons, which were sanctioned by the church authorities. Jesus was addressing that error.

> Jesus made it clear that God established marriage as a permanent relationship.

I believe that in dealing with marriage we should mix justice with mercy as Jesus exemplified so many times in his ministry. While we should endeavor to maintain the high ideal of marriage, we should deal mercifully with those who fail to do so. Every marriage has a set of circumstances which are unique. Our goal should be to rescue families rather than condemn them, especially while some are wrestling with the harsh emotional challenges that so many face in marriage today.

One of the prophets expressed the essence of Christian living in declaring a three-part prescription:

> He has showed you, o man, what is good; and what does the Lord
> require of you but
> * To do justice, and
> * To love kindness [mercy], and
> * To walk humbly with your God?[138]

Often those who claim to follow the Bible are excellent at emphasizing justice and humility before God but fail to practice the key element of mercy. Spouses, church leaders, and Christians need to practice this vital redemptive characteristic constantly in their homes and in their churches.

> The further we drift from God's creative design the more likely we are to end in conflict.

God Designed Male and Female

The creation account states that God created a man and a woman: "male and female created he them." He created them very differently for the purpose of complementing each other and for them to perform different functions in a united relationship. His design was perfect. However, sin intervened and not only

---

138 Micah, Chapter 6:8.

caused aberrations to develop resulting in disharmony in marriage relationships, but also a confusion of God's design for the role of the sexes. Consequently, the further we drift from God's creative design the more likely we are to end in conflict. Let's consider one difficult biblical passage, which appears to conflict with modern trends.

The problematic passage is found in Ephesians Chapter 5. It states:

> Wives, be subject to your husbands, as to the Lord. For the husband is
> head of the wife as Christ is head of the church, his body, and is
> himself the savior. As the Church is subject to Christ, so let wives be
> subject in everything to their husbands.[139]

The literal interpretation of this passage has dominated the view of marriage in western nations during the entire Christian era until recently. Men considered it their duty to dominate women through a patriarchal system. Women were not allowed to take a prominent role in society by voting or holding leading positions. They were paid less than men for the same work or they were not even allowed to enter some careers considered suitable only for men. Radical changes occurred in the second half of the last century that led to the open society of today.

The problem is that many men and women are still influenced by remnants of the old system. If the husband follows the old system and the wife considers herself liberated, conflict is inevitable until adjustments are made. That's what happened in our marriage.

In the past, ministers quoted Ephesians boldly during the wedding ceremony. Today, there is great reluctance to do so. As I consider the problematic passage, however, I do not see a real issue. I think it is a matter of context. It was not until late in my ministry that I noticed the previous verse, which states very clearly: "Be subject to one another...." Following the passage regarding the husband being the head of the wife are the words:

> Even so husbands should love their wives as their own bodies. He that
> loves his wife loves himself. For this reason a man shall leave his father
> and mother and be joined to his wife, and the two shall become one
> flesh.[140]

Notice the word "submit" used in the King James Version of the Bible instead of "subject" in the Revised Standard Version (Verse 21). If the Bible were directing

---

139 Ephesians, Chapter 5:22, 23.
140 Ephesians, Chapter 5:28, 31.

the husband to dominate his wife, it would be inconsistent since the command is for the husband to submit to his wife. Furthermore, the concept of becoming one body implies mutuality or unity in performing the functions of the body. To be consistent, the reference to the man being the head must be interpreted as function rather than status in the marital relationship. The metaphor considers the man as the head, the seat of reason. But should n't his wife be considered the heart, the source of passion and sustenance, the means by which the body is kept alive? The heart keeps the body, including the head, alive as it pumps blood, the life-giving source, to all the organs of the body. When the heart stops functioning, the body dies. There-fore, both the head and the heart serve vital, indispensable functions.

This passage is problematic not because it is obscure or appears to conflict with other passages of scripture but because our modern society considers it discriminatory against women. This passage is considered to perpetrate male dominance and female subservience. But does this passage do that? Absolutely not!

> The concept of becoming one body implies mutuality or unity in performing the functions of the body. To be consistent, the reference to the man being the head must be interpreted as function rather than status in the marital relationship.

Whenever we find a difficult passage in scripture, we must seek to understand it in the light of other passages in scripture and within its context. Now, the passage preceding it sets the basis of understanding for that which follows. It states, "Be subject to one another out of reverence for Christ." That is the missing link. The council is for both husbands and wives to respect each other's sphere of authority and influence and cooperate with each other. The passage ends with the words:

> ...let each one of you love his wife as himself, and let the wife see that she respects her husband.[141]

To the husband, the command is:

> Husbands, love your wives, as Christ loved the church and gave himself for it....He who loves his wife loves himself.[142]

---

141 Ephesians, Chapter 5:33.
142 Ephesians, Chapter 5:25, 28.

The Bible calls for hierarchy in the family, not one of dominance and subservience, but of role and function. Due to modern trends, the struggle over authority has plagued many homes, even Christian homes. William Hulme, a professor of pastoral counseling, puts it plainly:

> The Bible is more realistic about marriage than modern man, for the truth is that in dissolving the one hierarchy we dissolve the other.[143]

Professor Hulme adds:

> First the father was eliminated from family leadership and replaced by the mother. Now mother is being eliminated and the children are replacing her....But husband and wife may have to settle their own feud before they as parents can reassert parental leadership over the children.[144]

> The Bible calls for hierarchy in the family, not one of dominance and subservience but of role and function.

Husband's Role

The foregoing passage in Ephesians Chapter Five says, "For the husband is head of the wife as Christ is head of the Church" and "Husbands, love your wives as Christ loved the church." What, then, is Christ's relationship to the church? Therein lies the clues for the husband's conduct and the wife's response. Let's take a look at a few aspects of the relationship between Christ and his church.

> The family structure has some similarities to a well-run company.

• Leadership

From the Garden of Eden, God gave man authority and leadership. He assigned him the role of being in charge. The family structure has some similarities

---

143 William Hulme, "The Head of the House," *The Marriage Affair*, p. 73.
144 William Hulme, "The Head of the House," *The Marriage Affair*, pp. 73, 74.

to a well-run company. Someone must be in charge. If not, when an urgent decision is needed, confusion will result.

Let's take a glance at a firm founded by two partners. Both invest equal time and funds to start and run the company. Both agree to put their full time into the business to make it work. In order to succeed, they need to decide their functions in operating the business. They need to divide the responsibilities according to their talents and suitability for the various duties. Let me illustrate with a real experience.

Personal Story

It was 1958. Doug, a former schoolmate, and I decided to start a bottling company called Rainbow Manufacturing Company. We decided to produce new brands of syrup, vanilla, and soda. As recent high school graduates, we were novices to the business world. I had spent only three weeks in my first job as a bookkeeper in an auto parts firm, and Doug, who had graduated the previous year, worked on a farm for a year and for the previous three months he had worked as a salesman for a tractor company.

We reviewed our skills and interests. We agreed without any difficulty that Doug would be the president and I would be vice president of operations. He would deal with the staff and public relations and I would control the finances and distribution of the products. It was clearly understood without either of us mentioning it that we had equal ownership and consulted on major decisions. However, in the operational sphere, we were in control of the aspects of the business designated to us. We knew when to consult and when to act independently. After about a year, we sold out our interests to investors and went off to college. (By the way, we rose to become the third largest company among our eight competitors in that product line.) I don't recall any disagreement between us. The business operated smoothly and we became lifelong friends.

That is my understanding of the Ephesians passage. Both spouses have authority but the husband has leadership. Neither spouse should exercise control over the other. They are in partnership with different functions. For best results, each should operate in his/her own sphere with the interest of their partner at heart and they should collaborate when important decisions are needed. For marital harmony, each spouse should learn to complement the other.

I think we have inherited a corrupted version of the husband's authority from abuses that have occurred throughout history. In some cultures and political systems, men have dominated and exploited the women. That is certainly not the biblical model. The passage in Ephesians 5: 21 clearly states: "Be subject to *one another* out of reverence *for Christ*."

Have you noticed that Christ does not take away our freedom of choice? He invites us, entreats us, and even appeals to us to follow his directions. He does not force us to obey. Leadership means that the husband should take the lead preparing, protecting, and providing for the family at all times.

Let me illustrate. During the seventies when the women's movement was hitting its stride, I asked Pam if she wanted to be liberated. She replied unequivocally, NO! I was relieved, to say the least. I didn't understand any other role but to love, respect, protect, and cherish her as my wife. Today, I still delight to open doors for her at every opportunity. I drive her to work even though she has her own car. When we moved to Jacksonville from Nashville, after a brief search, we agreed on the house we wanted to buy. (Pam has the final say on that.) Then, I got to work to negotiate the contract, seek financing, and make all the other arrangements. I just kept her informed. I see my role as the provider and the one who takes the lead. It is true that in some marriages the balance of responsibilities may vary because of the different distribution of the talents of both spouses. However, the basic principle God established should remain as the framework of functioning: The husband leads and his wife exerts her influence as she supports him. It's a team experience.

> The basic principle God established should remain as the framework of functioning: The husband leads and his wife exerts her influence as she supports him. It's a team experience.

• Love

The command is for men to love their wives as Christ loved the Church. That love is not eros (human affection for each other). This is the real thing, the agape experience! This is the divine love which is expressed in I Corinthians, chapter 13.

- This love gives without expecting anything in return.
- This love sacrifices his life for the object of his love even when the person hates in return. It was while we were rebels against Christ that he died for us. While suffering the most painful death, he called out to his father to forgive his executioners. Even when our spouse is unlovable, we should still love.
- This love is patient and kind.
- This love does not insist on its own way. (Jesus gives us freedom to choose him or reject him. He never compels.)
- This love is also expressed sacrificially.

- A man should love purposefully. He expects his wife to respond to his love. Love is not fulfilled until it unites with its object.

Pastor Dwight Small, author of Design for Christian Marriage, says:

> Thus the lover is ever seeking a closer union of heart and life with his beloved. In the union of the two the meaning of life and love are realized. In Christian marriage the husband is ever to seek a deepening unity with his beloved in thought, expression, and in the shared life.[145]

To the man is given the command to love. Love is built into the very nature of women. That's their secret weapon. They reveal it in grace and charm and empathy that men can only strive to achieve.

• Sacrifice

Pastor Dwight Small adds this thought:

> Husbands must love their wives sacrificially. They must be willing to give up all that is required to fulfill the life of the beloved. This may involve giving up some of their interests, their time, their pleasures, their ambitions and their friends. It means that nothing shall have priority over their responsibility to fulfill the needs of their wives. There is no substitute for the giving of oneself.[146]

• Peter's Counsel (1 Peter Chapter Three)

Peter is admonishing both husband and wife concerning their relationship with each other. I find in this passage several gems for husbands and wives. To the husbands, Peter says:

- Live considerately with your wife.
- Bestow honor on your wife.
- You are both joint heirs of the grace of life (shared life).
- Your spiritual growth is determined by how you treat your wife.
- God may not even answer your prayers if, as her husband, you fail to care for your wife.

---

145 Dwight Small, "The Lover," *The Marriage Affair.*, p. 86.
146 Dwight Small, "The Lover," *The Marriage Affair*, p. 85.

To the wives, Peter says:

- Be supportive (submissive) to your husbands.
- Use your internal graces to influence and win over your husband.
- Depend more on your inner quality rather than outer adornment.

> A woman has some qualities that men cannot easily replicate. Whereas the man uses authority to achieve his goals, the woman uses influence.

Wife's Role

Influence

A woman has some qualities that men cannot easily replicate. Whereas the man uses authority to achieve his goals, the woman uses influence. For much of our marriage, Pam warned me about the influence women can have over me. I didn't take her seriously until I decided to experiment. I won't try that again.

I had just finished a board meeting. A young lady, who was a prominent member of my congregation, lingered behind until I was alone in the room. She was very direct. She told me that she was in love with me. I was completely committed to my wife and had no desire to break that commitment. However, as I regained my composure, I decided to allow the friendship to develop with a clear understanding with her that we would not engage in anything that would violate our commitment to our spouses. I just wanted to know whether I could be close to a woman without sexual involvement. I escaped from that situation eventually without capitulation. However, I decided then that a woman's influence is indeed more than most men imagine.

Remember the saying, "The hand that rocks the cradle rules the world." Believe it. Not only do mothers provide a foundation for their children to achieve greatness later in life, but many great men have fallen prey to the spell of influential women. Women can exude a grace and charm that most men find irresistible.

Under such charming influence of women, some men agree to do things they would not do under normal circumstances. Take the biblical Samson, for instance. He surrendered his power, strength, and freedom under the charm of a woman. Unfortunately, much more is said of the negative influence of women than the positive outcome of their influence. Because of the corrupting impact of sex in our society, when we think of the influence of women we tend to think of the billboards, television advertising, and Hollywood movies.

History is replete with the acts of women who use their influence positively. Many of their heroic tales have never been told. Can we think of the number of women who have influenced national policies through their husbands who serve as kings and presidents?

Abigail's Influence

Let me tell the story of a woman in the Bible who changed the mind of a king in waiting. I could use Ruth's subtle influence with Boaz or Esther's influence over King Ahasuerus in her heroic effort to save the Jewish people. Instead, I have chosen the lesser known Abigail.

It happened during the time when Saul and David were feuding. God had chosen David as Saul's successor as King of Israel. King Saul, jealous of David's growing influence, was seeking to take his life. David and his soldiers were in the region of Carmel where a wealthy man named Nabal kept his flock. David and his men needed supplies. He sent ten men to request help from Nabal rather than taking his goods by force. Nabal despised them and sent them away with the words:

> Who is David? Who is the son of Jesse? There are many servants
> nowadays who are breaking away from their masters. Shall I take
> my bread and my water and my meat that I have killed for my shearers,
> and give it to men who come from I do not know where?[147]

When David's servants returned with that disdainful message, David was angry. So David armed himself, took four hundred of his men, and started on the way to destroy Nabal and his servants. When Abigail,
Nabal's wife, heard what her husband said, she decided to intervene privately. Taking an abundant supply of food, she hastened to meet David. She carried two hundred loaves of bread, two jugs of wine, five roasted sheep, five measures of parched grain, a hundred clusters of raisins, and two hundred cakes of figs.

Upon meeting David on the way, Abigail descended from the ass she was riding and bowed before David. She proceeded to give a moving apology for her husband and offered the gifts in appeasement. David accepted her gracious gesture and the generous gift and was turned away from his wrath against Nabal. David said:

---

147 1 Samuel, Chapter 25:10, 11.

> Blessed be the Lord, the God of Israel, who sent you this day to meet
> me! Blessed be your discretion, and blessed be you, who have kept me
> this day from bloodguilt and from avenging myself with my own hand.
> For as sure as the Lord God of Israel lives, who has restrained me from
> hurting you, unless you had made haste and come to meet me, truly by
> morning there had not been left to Nabal so much as one male. Go up
> in peace to your house; see, I have harkened to your voice, and I have
> granted your petition.[148]

The story would have been remarkable enough if it ended there. However, what added to its intrigue are the events which followed. The following morning Abigail told her husband about what David swore to do and what she had done to avert the impending calamity. The record says that Nabal's "heart died within him, and he became as a stone."

He died ten days later, perhaps from a heart attack. When David realized that the Lord had avenged him and Abigail had saved him from taking vengeance himself, he was pleased. In fact, David was so pleased and impressed with Abigail's charm and influence that he invited her to become his wife. By using her influence positively, Abigail not only saved her household but became known through history as Queen Abigail. Can you imagine her influence on King David during his reign?

According to Peter, a wise woman will endure the problems brought on by her unconverted husband.[149] By using her feminine graces, she may win him to herself and to Christ. We may recall the virtues of a good wife as presented in the last chapter of Proverbs. Abigail seems to have matched Solomon's description of an ideal wife.

Support

The Ephesians passage we discussed above clearly counsels the wife to support her husband. He thrives on affirmation from his wife. Many wives fail to understand the importance of any encouragement they offer their husbands. Even worse, some wives replace encouragement with criticism. Regardless of how men appear to be self-sufficient and self-assured, they welcome and even thrive on support and encouragement from their wives.

---

148 1 Samuel, Chapter 25:32-35.
149 1 Peter, Chapter 3:1-6.

> Regardless of how men appear to be self-sufficient and selfassured, they welcome and even thrive on support and encouragement from their wives.

Respond

Whereas the husband's role is to lead, the wife's role is to respond. The woman is given the exalted role of being compared to the Church, which is called the bride of Christ. As Christians we are called upon to respond to Christ's leading in order that we may unite with Christ in the home he has gone to prepare.

In an earlier chapter, I related the story about my father and his second wife. My mother had passed away leaving three small children to his care. His new wife acted very independently. She acted as though the only things that mattered were the care for her son and her own well-being. She failed to make decisions with my father's future or our family's well-being in her plans.

Since my father could not find work in the small district where we lived, he invited his wife to move with him to a larger town not very far away where jobs were available. She refused. He moved in order to work to provide for us. He took my older sister with him and sent me to live with my grandmother. My brother, the eldest, remained in the house alone to care for himself at age fifteen. My father returned to visit on weekends but the arrangement was doomed to fail. Both of them lost. She bemoaned her loneliness and died blaming my father for failing to love and care for her the way she expected. His need for companionship led him to form another relationship with a woman who eventually became his third wife. How different their lives and ours could have been if my father and his second wife had only been able to find a way to be together. My first stepmother was supportive of my father and they appeared to love each other, but when she declined his invitation to relocate due to necessity, any hope of building a lasting marriage was dashed. The long-distance love affair waned.

God Invented Sex

Some Christians think of sex as part of the sin problem. They consider sex as the opposite of a spiritual life. But it was God who invented sex. Sin corrupted the sanctity of sex. In the first chapter of Genesis, God said to Adam and Eve, "Be fruitful and multiply, and fill the earth."[150]

Here, God authorized sex as a part of normal functioning. The Scriptures further state that marriage should be held in high honor and the marriage bed should be undefiled.[151]

---

150 Genesis, Chapter 1:28.
151 Hebrews, Chapter 13:4.

Sex within marriage is wholesome and desirable but sex outside of marriage is condemned as fornication or adultery. Paul's counsel concerning sex is:

> The husband should give to his wife her conjugal rights
> [sexual rights], and likewise the wife to her husband.
> For the wife does not rule over her own body, but the
> husband does; likewise the husband does not rule over
> his own body, but the wife does. Do not refuse one
> another except by agreement for a season....[152]

Marriage has a built-in understanding that sex between the spouses should be encouraged mutually. Circumstances such as illness or fatigue may cause one partner to lack desire for sex temporarily when the other partner has the desire. That is understandable. However, when one partner unilaterally declines sex for selfish reasons, as punishment, or through resentment, the Bible condemns such a conduct. Unless there is common agreement between the spouses, both should feel constrained to consider the others' need for sex as important.

Sex within marriage is wholesome and desirable but sex outside of marriage is condemned as fornication or adultery.

Pointing out that our bodies are temples of God, Paul says:

> Every other sin which a man commits is outside the body; but the
> immoral man sins against his own body.[153]

The Bible frequently and fiercely condemns the violation of the proper use of sex. The Bible warns against promiscuity, sexual deviancy, and adultery. Your body should be treated as the temple of God, a place where God resides.

In translations from the New Testament's original Greek language, the English word "temple" often replaces different words in biblical Greek. For instance, one word was used when the Greeks meant the whole temple complex with its various

---

152 1 Corinthians, Chapter 7:3-5.
153 1 Corinthians, Chapter 6:18.

compartments and a different word was used to describe the sanctuary where the priests offered sacrifices.

> Our bodies should be treated with the understanding that we are made in the image of God and our bodies should be kept from pollution of any sort illicit drugs, unhealthy foods, harmful practices, immoral conduct, and unlawful sexual practices.

Which word do you think Paul used to describe our bodies? If you guessed the temple itself (naos), you are right. In Paul's time, non-Jewish worshippers used this word to describe the part of the temple or shrine where they placed their gods. Our bodies should be treated with the understanding that we are made in the image of God and our bodies should be kept from pollution of any sort illicit drugs, unhealthy foods, harmful practices, immoral conduct, and unlawful sexual practices.

Those who search the Bible for principles to guide their lives cannot miss the significance God places on sexual conduct. Let me explain briefly. The record states that the Christians who lived in the corrupt city of Corinth had a serious debate about how to relate to sex as Christians. They wrote to Paul for guidance. We don't know the exact questions but we can determine them from the answer Paul gave. Here is the issue.

Since the belly was made for food and food for the belly, should we not conclude that the same applies to sex? The male and female sexual organs were made to pleasure each other. Should we not be free to fulfill the function for which sexual organs are made?[154] (See I Corinthians 6). Paul's answer is direct and incisive. True! The sexual organs were made for sex but if you fail to use them with moral restraint, God will destroy both the sexual organs and the immoral performers of sex. Paul further asserts that God considers sexual immorality to be worse than other sins. Unlike other sins such as lying, stealing, killing, in which the mind and limbs are used to carry them out, the whole body itself is used as the instrument of sexual immorality.

God Taught Forgiveness

Even though the Bible allows for divorce when adultery is committed by one partner, there is a provision for forgiveness and healing. God commissioned the prophet Hosea to take back his wife who had been unfaithful. His example would

---

154 1 Corinthians, Chapter 6:12-16.

illustrate how God deals with his people who rebelled against him. Even though we have gone astray, God seeks after us and draws us back to him. So also we should be patient and forgiving with our spouses when they wrong us.

> When couples are engaged in a mission of service to others, they generate a new passion as they see results and enjoy real satisfaction.

Service

During our forty-plus years of marriage, Pam and I have focused on service. In fact, we consider our emphasis on service to be indispensable to the success of our marriage. If we had spent much of our time seeking pleasure or focusing on ourselves, we might have been bored long ago. We found that as we paid attention to others, we renewed our passion for life and each other.

> We found that as we paid attention to others, we renewed our passion for life and each other.

In his book The Seven Principles of Making Marriage Work, Dr. John Gottman called the development of a family culture "creating shared meaning". Developing interest in service to others does create shared meaning. This emphasis provides a basis for sharing passion toward achieving a common goal. As human beings, we seem to thrive when we hitch our wagons to a star. We need a sense of connectedness to something bigger than ourselves. Those who spend their time in seeking self-pleasure may soon dissipate their energies in evaporating emotions. They are left with an empty feeling that desires more and more of the same. They may end up blaming or nagging their spouses for trivial causes. When couples are engaged in a mission of service to others, they generate a new passion as they see results and enjoy real satisfaction.

Some authors such as Dr. Jean Baker Miller consider women as naturally more inclined to give sacrificially than men. Men are more focused on task and achievement. Women activists seek to liberate women from this built-in desire to serve. Since they are usually more caring, nurturing, and giving, they need to seek to free themselves from this burden. These authors feel that women reap less praise for their sacrifice than men do, since they are considered the class of givers. Dr. Jean Baker Miller declares:

Women do have a much greater and refined ability to encompass others' needs and to do this with ease. By this I mean that women are better geared than men to first recognize others' needs and then to believe strongly that others' needs can be served that they can respond to others' needs without feeling this as a detraction from their sense of identity.[155]

She points out that women's sacrificial service is not problematic per se but becomes a problem when they are forced by society into subservient roles. I have no doubt that when husband and wife engage in shared service or shared giving they enhance their relationship and enrich their lives together. Ellen White writes:

The pleasure of doing good animates the mind and vibrates through the whole body. While the faces of the benevolent men are lighted up with cheerfulness, and their countenances express the moral elevation of the mind, those of selfish stingy men are dejected, cast down, and gloomy....Real happiness is found only in being good and doing good. The highest enjoyment comes to those who faithfully fulfill their appointed duties.[156]

I am convinced that when both spouses share a genuine spiritual basis for their lives and commit themselves to giving generously and performing service to others, they increase their chances of enjoying a happy and successful relationship together for life.

---

155 Jean Baker Miller, *Toward A New Psychology of Women*, p. 61.
156 Ellen G. White, *Messages to Young People*, pp. 209, 210.

Conclusion

It is not uncommon for people to know what they need to do but fail to do it even though they realize it would yield them significant benefits. That's what happened to me during much of my marriage. I knew what I should do to make my wife and children happy but often I found myself unable to overcome certain built-in feelings or habits that created a barrier between knowing and performing.

I don't think I am alone. Think of the number of people who know and are even convinced that a consistent exercise program is good for their health, but they watch their health decline while they complain every day about their maladies. They are fully convinced these ailments would diminish or disappear if they spent a mere ten minutes a few times per week exercising. But they don't! Something subtle deep within the psyche registers the messages: Don't do it today, I am tired; I am too busy; my poor body won't be able to endure it; I have lots of things I can do with the time I would spend exercising; I will start during my holidays.

> I knew what I should do to make my wife and children happy but often I found myself unable to overcome certain built-in feelings or habits that created a barrier between knowing and performing.

At the age of twenty-seven, I woke up one morning and could not climb out of bed. My body felt like a log and I just wanted to lie there. The problem was I had to go to work. I knew I wasn't sick because otherwise I felt fine. So I made a rash decision. Without debating with myself, I decided to begin an exercise program immediately.

I placed one arm over the edge of the bed, then a leg, and then I rolled my whole body off the bed. I struggled to my feet, put on a pair of shorts and a sweat shirt. Then I went on the street for a jog. The problem was that all the dogs in the area barked at me or ran along the fence as if to challenge me to a fierce battle. After a few mornings of dogs howling in my ears, I confined myself to the tiny backyard and ran in circles.

After that early beginning, I moved to Canada where the weather was inimical during much of the year. I didn't want to pay the exorbitant cost of a regular gym or take the time to travel to a gym (although I did that a few times over the years). I vowed to jog four times per week whether there is sun, snow, or sleet. More recently, I bought an exercise machine, placed it in the garage and continued my exercise four times per week.

Ever since that fateful morning when I could not get out of bed, I rarely, if ever, feel tired in the mornings. When my eyes open every morning, my entire body leaps up and I am ready to go. I don't know what illegal drugs are like because I have never taken any of them, but after I exercise each day, my body feels like energy is being pumped into my system as if I have taken some kind of energy-generating elixir.

> It is difficult to do some things that are necessary for our well- being, such as changing our behavior and attitude to our spouses, follow a healthy lifestyle, or managing our money. But it takes a commitment and a determination to stick with it. Don't argue with yourself, temporize, or spend time planning. Just do it!

Now, more than thirty-eight years later, I am still following my exercise routine. In addition, from age eighteen, I have avoided fatty meats, alcohol, drinks with caffeine, and smoking. More recently, I have been committed to consistently contributing to my wife's happiness and to live debt free.

It is difficult to do some things that are necessary for our well-being, such as changing our behavior and attitude to our spouse, follow a healthy lifestyle, or managing our money. But it takes a commitment and a determination to stick with it. Don't argue with yourself, temporize, or spend time planning. Just do it!

Those who have faith can rely on God's help in achieving their goal. Those without a religious faith need to pray Peter's prayer as he faced certain death in the turbulent water which threatened to overwhelm him. This may be the shortest prayer in the Bible. In desperation, Peter exclaimed, "Lord save me!"

Jesus did. He still does. Remember: The decision of a moment can change the destiny of a lifetime.

The Challenge of Growth

Dr. Oliver Wendell Holmes, the nineteenth-century physician, essayist, and poet, penned a poem that has inspired me from college days. Dr. Wendell Holmes likely read Ralph Waldo Emerson's observation concerning the growth of a certain shellfish. He adapted it to the poem, which has influenced many lives. In 1858, he wrote the poem entitled "The Chambered Nautilus." The example of the shellfish provides a magnificent lesson for us. We all need to challenge ourselves. Fortunately, divine help is available to everyone.

Ralph Waldo Emerson had observed how the shellfish crawled out of its comfortable, secure shell when it outgrew it and exposed itself to the harsh forces of nature while it formed a new, roomier, and more beautiful shell to accommodate its growth and protect its delicate body. Using this striking metaphor, Dr. Oliver Wendell Holmes writes:

> Build thee more stately mansions, o my soul,
> As the swift seasons roll!
> Leave thy low-vaulted past!
> Let each new temple, nobler than the last,
> Shut thee from heaven with a dome more vast,
> Till thou at length art free,
> Leaving thine outgrown shell by life's unresting sea!

May those who read this book challenge themselves, like the shellfish, to attain unparalleled growth in their personal lives and in their relationships.

Let me conclude with marriage advice from a counselor who was taught by Jesus. In 1 Peter, Chapter 3:8-12, Peter declares:

> Finally, all of you, have unity of spirit, sympathy, love of the brethren,
> a tender heart, and a humble mind. Do not return evil for evil or
> reviling for reviling; but on the contrary bless, for to this you have
> been called, that you may obtain a blessing. For he that would love
> life and see good days, let him keep his tongue from evil and his lips
> from speaking guile; let him turn away from evil and do right; let him
> seek peace and pursue it. For the eyes of the Lord are upon the righteous,
> and his ears are open to their prayer.

Bibliography

Auldrich, Sandra P. Men Read Newspapers, Not Minds. Wheaton, Illinois: Tyndale House Publishers, 1996.

Begg, Alistair. Lasting Love. Chicago: Moody Press, 1997.

Bennett, William J. The Broken Hearth. New York: Doubleday, 2001.

Betcher, William and Macauley, Robie. The Seven Basic Quarrels of Marriage. New York: Villard Books, 1990.

Boyd, Neil. The Beast Within: Why Men Are Violent. New York: Greystone Books, 2000.

Brody, Steve and Brody, Cathy. Renew Your Marriage at Midlife. New York: G. P. Putnam's Sons, 1999.

Campbell, Anne. Men, Women, and Aggression. New York: Basic Books, 1993. Carroll, Ted. Live Debt Free. Avon, MA: Adams Media, 2004.
Cohen, Eric. J. and Sterling, Gregory. You Owe Me. New Jersey: New Horizon Press, 1999.

Cohen, Robert Stephen. Reconcilable Differences. New York: Pocket Books, 2002. Conway, Jim. Men in Midlife. Colorado: Chariot Victor Publishing, 1997.
Davis, Michelle Weiner. The Sex-Starved Marriage. New York: Simon & Schuster, 2003.

DeAngelis, Barbara. What Women Want Men to Know. New York: Hyperion, 2001.

Dobson, James. Marriage and Family. Wheaton, Illinois: Tyndale Publishing, 2000.

Doyle, Laura. The Surrendered Wife. New York: Simon & Schuster, 2001.

Ellis, Albert and Crawford, Ted. Making Intimate Connections. CA.: Impact Publishing, Inc., 2000.

Eldridge, John. You Have What It Takes. Nashville: Nelson Books, 2004.

Fein, Ellen and Schneider, Sherrie. The Rules for Marriage. New York: Warner Books, 2001.

Ferrebee, Louise, General Editor. The Healthy Marriage Handbook. Tennessee: Broadman & Holman Publishing Co., 2001.

Garcia-Pratts, Catherine Musco and Joseph A. Good Marriages Don't Just Happen. Texas, Thomas Moore, 2000.
George, Stephen C. et al. A Lifetime of Sex. Pennsylvania: Rodale Press, 1998. Glasser, William and Carleen. Getting Together and Staying Together. New York: HarperCollins, 2000.

Gottman, John. Why Marriages Succeed or Fail? New York: Simon & Schuster, 1994.

Gottman, John. The Seven Principles of Making Marriage Work. New York: Crown Publishers, 1999.

Gray, John. Men Are from Mars, Women Are from Venus. New York: HarperCollins, 1992.

Harley Jr. Willard F. His Needs, Her Needs. Grand Rapids, MI.: Fleming H. Revell, 1994.

Janus, Samuel S. and Cynthia. The Janus Report. New York: John Wiley and Sons, 1993.

Kelly, Linda. Two Incomes and Still Broke. New York: Random House, 1996. Krasnow, Iris. Surrendering to Marriage. New York: Hyperion Press, 2001.

Leiblum, Sandra and Sacks, Judith. Getting the Sex You Want. New York: Crown, 2002.

Lerner, Harriett. The Dance of Anger. New York: HarperCollins, 1997. Lister, Pamela. Married Sex. New York: Hearst Books, 2001.
Lowery, Fred. Covenant Marriage. West Monroe, LA.: Howard Publishing, 2002.

Mundis, Jerrold. How to Get Out of Debt, Stay Out of Debt, and Live Prosperously. New York: Bantam Books, 2003.

Petersen, J. Allan. For Men Only. Wheaton, Il.: Tyndale Publishers, 1973. Petersen, J. Allan. The Marriage Affair. Wheaton, Il.: Tyndale House, 1971. Ramsay, Dave. Financial Peace. New York: Viking Penguin Books, 1995.
Rheims, Diane and John. Toward Commitment. New York: Alfred K. Knoff, 2002.

Samms, Robert. Making Marriage Meaningful. Lincoln, NE.: iUniverse, 2005. Schnarch, David. Passionate Marriage. New York: Henry Holt & Co., 1997. Schnarch, David. Resurrecting Sex. New York: HarperCollins, 2002.
Stanley, Scott. The Heart of Commitment. Nashville: Thomas Nelson Publishers, 1998.

Townsend, John. What Women Want, What Men Want. Oxford: Oxford University Press, 1999.

Van Pelt, Nancy. To Have and to Hold. Nashville: Southern Publishing, 1980.

Van Pelt, Nancy. We've Only Just Begun. Hagerstown, MD.: Review Herald, 1985.

Wallerstein, Judith and Blakeslee, Sandra. The Good Marriage. New York: Houghton Mifflin Co., 1995.

Wetzler, Scott. Living With the Passive-Aggressive Man. New York: Fireside Publishing, 1992.

White, Ellen G. Messages to Young People. Nashville: Southern Publishing, 1974.

Other Sources

Advent Review (periodical). Hagerstown, MD.

Atlanta Journal-Constitution (newspaper). Atlanta, GA.
Psychology Today. Okemos, MI. Quest, Canada's urban magazine. Redbook. New York, New York.

Statistical Abstract of the United States, U. S. Census Bureau, 2004–2005.
Statistics Canada.
The Sunday Gleaner (newspaper). Jamaica.
The Paducah Sun (newspaper). Paducah, KY.
The Tormont Webster's Illustrated Encyclopedic Dictionary. Montreal: Tormont Publications, 1990.

U. S. Census Bureau, 2000.
Vital Statistics of the United States. U. S. Department of Health and Human Services, 1985.

www.ingramcontent.com/pod-product-compliance
Lightning Source LLC
Chambersburg PA
CBHW080622030426
42336CB00018B/3050